Robert Earle Morgan
Wingate College
Wingate, North Carolina

In the forecourt of the Lincoln National Life Insurance Building in Fort Wayne, Indiana, stands the unusual "Statue of Lincoln as a Boy" by Paul Manship. Housed in the building, and supported by the Lincoln National Life Foundation, is the Museum of Lincoln Lore, one of the most important libraries of Lincolniana in the United States.

MARKS OF LINCOLN

ON OUR LAND

MAURINE WHORTON REDWAY

AND

DOROTHY KENDALL BRACKEN

Marks of Lincoln

on Our Land

HASTINGS HOUSE, PUBLISHERS, NEW YORK

Library of Congress Catalog Card Number: 57-8642

Published simultaneously in Canada by
S. J. Reginald Saunders, Publishers, Toronto 2B

Printed in the United States of America

FOR AMERICANS

To encourage the study and veneration

of our historic shrines.

PREFACE

Marks of Lincoln on Our Land is a study in pictures of the life of Abraham Lincoln—an extraordinary life which became a unique chapter in history and which has been recorded across our country in a phenomenal number of landmarks, statues and memorials. These shrines and markers which posterity has erected to honor the Great Emancipator have followed in his wake wherever he went in his brilliant rise from log cabin to White House, from rural obscurity to Presidency, from frontier innocence to national tragedy.

This pictorial treasury has a three-fold purpose: to serve as a guide book to the markers and memorials themselves; to relate in its essential outline the story of Lincoln's life, which is, indeed, most interestingly traced in the very events the memorials commemorate; and finally, to stimulate its readers to travel in person the historic trail of the Lincoln monuments.

This collection does not purport to be absolutely complete, nor does it presume to be a work of pedantic scholarship. But considerable research and a great deal of travel have gone into this graphic guide to Lincoln's inspiring life. The authors have followed each picture with a description of the shrine, monument or building illustrated, and with an historical flashback to the period of Lincoln's life which relates to that place. The narrative begins at his humble birthplace near Hodgenville, Kentucky; each subsequent memorial mark on our land turns another page in this noble life history, until a grandiose climax is reached in the tremendous classic structure of the Lincoln Memorial in Washington, D. C.—the ultimate tribute of Americans to Abe Lincoln's great personal achievement and to his inestimable services to our beloved country.

The authors sincerely hope that *Marks of Lincoln on Our Land* will lead its readers to days of memorable travel and inspire them to read further, in the numerous treasures of Lincoln literature, about the boy of the cabins who became a Man of the Ages.

ACKNOWLEDGMENTS

Miss Donna Muegge, Secretary, Chamber of Commerce, Quincy, Ill.

Frederick Tilberg, Historian, Gettysburg National Military Park, Gettysburg, Pa.

Mrs. Bess V. Ehrmann, Chairman, Village Committee, Rockport, Ill.

Dan B. Whorton, Private Secretary, Sweetwater, Texas.

The late Harry E. Pratt, Illinois State Historical Library, Springfield, Ill.

Mrs. Grace Middleton, Hodgenville, Ky.

John Hall Jacobs, Librarian, New Orleans Public Library, New Orleans, La.

Ernest L. Wright, Jr., Superintendent, Abraham Lincoln National Historical Park, Hodgenville, Ky.

P. J. Rinderle, Director of Publicity, Chamber of Commerce, New Orleans, La.

Robert J. Reynolds, Illustrations Staff, *The National Geographic* Magazine, Washington, D. C.

Mrs. Lia Schipper, Secretary to Sales Manager, Rutgers University, New Brunswick, N. J.

Russell Laird, Superintendent, Lincoln State Memorial Park, Lincoln City, Ind.

Springfield, Ill.

Miss Virginia Daiker, Reference Librarian, The Library of Congress, Washington, D. C.

R. Gerald McMurtry, Director, The Lincoln National Life Foundation, Fort Wayne, Ind.

Mrs. Helen C. Braack, Librarian, Woodrow Wilson High School, Dallas, Texas.

René Ballard, Director of Public Relations, Knox College, Galesburg, Ill.

Mrs. Karin Spachman, Secretary, Public Relations Office, Knox College, Galesburg, Ill.

Mrs. Helen L. Snyder, Secretary, Gettysburg Chamber of Commerce, Gettysburg, Pa.

PHOTOGRAPHIC CREDITS

Department of the Interior, National Capital Parks,
    National Park Service, Washington, D. C.

Abbie Rowe, Department of the Interior, National Capital Parks,
    National Park Service, Washington, D. C.

Clifford F. Bracken, Photographer, Dallas, Texas

Ray E. White Photo Service, Quincy, Ill.

Bill Wood Photo Company, Fort Worth, Texas.

The Lane Studio, Gettysburg, Pa.

Howard E. Gardner, Hodgenville, Ky.

Herbert Georg Studio, Springfield, Ill.

Library of Congress, Photoduplication Service, Washington, D. C.

Chicago Park District, Chicago, Ill.

The Lincoln National Life Foundation, Fort Wayne, Ind.

Fred T. Colwell, Washington Board of Trade, Washington, D. C.

Wide World Photos, Inc., New York, N. Y.

CONTENTS

13 MARKS OF LINCOLN ON OUR LAND

MARKS OF LINCOLN

ON OUR LAND

STATUE OF ABRAHAM LINCOLN

Hodgenville, Kentucky

Abraham Lincoln, of lowly birth, lofty purpose, and supreme accomplishment, truly "belongs to the ages." Rarely in American history has a patriot started with so little and achieved so much. Annually millions of Americans make pilgrimages to his hallowed birthplace in Kentucky, to his numerous abodes in Indiana and Illinois, and to places he frequented in and around Washington, D. C. His humble birth, his laborious climb to statesmanship, and his fervent belief in the preservation of the Union have inspired his countrymen to commemorate the marks of Lincoln on our land.

SINKING SPRING

Along Lincoln Boulevard, three miles south of Hodgenville, a split-rail fence encloses the Abraham Lincoln National Historical Park, which includes one hundred acres of the original Thomas Lincoln farm and memorializes the birthplace of Abraham Lincoln. In 1808 Thomas Lincoln, eighth owner of the Sinking Spring farm, paid $200 for the 348.5-acre tract and signed a title lien for $51.50. Soon Thomas and Nancy Hanks Lincoln and their daughter Sarah moved into their crude log cabin. There, on February 12, 1809, Abraham Lincoln was born during a fearful blizzard. In 1816, by foreclosure and public auction, Thomas Lincoln, who had already moved his family to his Knob Creek home, lost the Sinking Spring farm. During the following century a succession of owners sold, reduced and neglected the Sinking Spring farm and permitted the birthplace cabin to be moved away.

Between 1905 and 1916 the Lincoln Farm Association, fortified with funds of more than $350,000 in donations from American citizens and school children, bought the park land,

Sinking Spring, Lincoln National Historical Park,
Hodgenville, Kentucky

reclaimed the alleged Lincoln cabin from its uncertain years of intermittent storage and exhibition, constructed the handsome Memorial Building to shelter the cabin, and beautified the site. In 1916 the Association deeded to the United States the park area of 110.5 acres, together with its buildings and an endowment fund of $48,000 for further maintenance and improvements.

The Abraham Lincoln National Historical Park, administered by the National Park Service, admirably preserves Abraham Lincoln's first imprints on a pioneer land. Most notable are the protected Sinking Spring, a giant white oak tree, and the granite shrine which shields the traditional cabin in which Abe Lincoln was born. In and around this area Lincoln spent the first two years of his rugged life.

The famous Sinking Spring is encased in a stone wall and is reached by a cobblestone path. Recessed in cool limestone and variously known as Cave Spring and Rock Spring, Sinking Spring gave its name to the farm of Abe Lincoln's nativity. From this faithful spring the Lincoln family obtained a pure drinking supply and young Abe got his earliest sips of cold water.

This historic spring and the huge white oak, nearly three hundred years old, are the natural reminders of Lincoln's life on this farm. The Boundary Oak, a landmark for the early white settlers, was a marker in the original 1805 grant that later included the Thomas Lincoln farm. This giant tree, nearly one hundred feet high, is the sole survivor of all that was living here when Abe Lincoln was born. It once sheltered the youth's early home and now majestically points upward to the magnificent shrine that towers over the humble Lincoln cabin.

More enduring than the Sinking Spring, the majestic tree, or the magnificent Lincoln Memorial, this hallowed ground itself transcends water, wood and stone and speaks a living message to all Americans of the mystery of life and the majesty of achievement. For here was born the man who reasoned, "Why should there not be a patient confidence in the justice of the people? Is there any better hope in the world?"

Lincoln Memorial, Lincoln National Historical Park, *Hodgenville, Kentucky*

LINCOLN MEMORIAL

Hodgenville, Kentucky

The Lincoln Memorial, erected on or near the original site of the birthplace cabin, is a magnificent tribute to the pioneer who became President. Built by nation-wide contributions of $250,000, this granite temple surmounts the landscape of terraced walks, the Sinking Spring, and the Boundary Oak. During seven years of construction this impressive shrine was fashioned from Kentucky granite and pink Connecticut marble. Everything in and around it commemorates the rustic birthplace of Abe Lincoln, lowly in origin and tragic in eminence.

From a gentle vale fifty-six terraced steps, symbolic of the mortal years of the martyred President, lead up to the Memorial which is embellished on all four walls by stately granite Doric columns. At the front, six columns form a lofty portico which shields massive double doors of bronze. Inscribed on the imposing façade and engraved on bronze plaques on both the interior and the exterior of the Memorial are excerpts of Lincoln's public addresses that are familiar to all American school children. At the front portal the bronze plaque on the right states:

> Stand with anybody that stands right. Stand with him while he is right, and part with him while he is wrong. Peoria, Ill.   Oct. 16, 1854.

The bronze plaque on the left states:

> Let us have faith that right makes might, and in that faith let us to the end dare to do our duty as we understand it. Cooper Institute, N. Y.   Feb. 27, 1860.

During the twentieth century three Presidents have memorialized this hallowed shrine which commemorates the humble birthplace of President Lincoln who toiled to save the Union. In 1909, a century after Abe Lincoln's life began on this raw Kentucky frontier, President Theodore Roosevelt laid the cornerstone of the Lincoln Memorial to honor the giant Rail Splitter. Two years later President William Howard

Lincoln Birthplace Cabin, Lincoln National Historical Park,
Hodgenville, Kentucky

Taft dedicated the edifice, memorializing the statesman whose words and deeds helped "to weld a divided nation and to bind up a nation's wounds." Finally, in 1916 President Woodrow Wilson delivered the acceptance oration at the completed Memorial, commemorating Abraham Lincoln's laborious rise from a lowly origin to the Presidency which culminated in his triumphant martyrdom for our nation's "new birth of freedom."

LINCOLN BIRTHPLACE CABIN

Enshrined in the classic Memorial Building of granite and marble, the traditional Abraham Lincoln birthplace cabin is preserved for posterity by the National Park Service. This single-room log cabin, with a crude chimney, one door and a small window, sheltered the Thomas Lincoln family from 1809 to 1811, during Abe's infancy.

The Lincoln cabin has endured many changes. After Thomas Lincoln took his family to Knob Creek and lost the Sinking Spring by foreclosure, the old cabin was variously used as a tenant house and a schoolroom. During 1897 the historic cabin was dismantled and its logs were numbered, and it became a meandering exhibit feature in various American cities. In 1906 the famous cabin was purchased by the Lincoln Farm Association and sent to Louisville, Kentucky, where it was intermittently stored and exhibited pending the completion of the Memorial Building. Finally, in 1911, the traditional cabin was transported to the birthplace farm and re-erected inside the magnificent shrine. The old cabin, slightly smaller than the original, now measures 13 by 17 feet, and several new logs replace deteriorated timbers.

Thus a classic building of stone protects the humble birthplace of a great statesman. With striking contrast, an architectural gem enshrines a primitive log cabin. The interior of the shrine has simple lines of classic grandeur; with great dignity it encloses the lowly cabin built in the rustic mode of primitive necessity. Near the front portal, the white marble and granite walls of the Memorial Building are embellished with the stirring words of Lincoln's Gettysburg Address. On the left side of the rear doorway an engraved panel holds the

Knob Creek Farm (Lincoln's boyhood home), near Hodgenville, Kentucky

terse autobiography of Abraham Lincoln which he told when he was pressed about his early life; on the right a panel of poetry by Maurice Thompson and Edwin Markham gives an abiding appraisal and characterization of Lincoln, the great American. In the lofty ceiling the sixteen rosettes carved in stone are symbolic of Lincoln as our sixteenth President.

The interior of the log cabin is rough and unfinished, in the traditional manner of humble pioneer folk. The puncheon floor, the mud-chinked walls, the crude chimney and stone hearth, the poles for the loft, and the supports for the rived shingle roof each day graphically remind the visiting throngs of Lincoln's lowly beginnings.

The sheltering shrine is impressive evidence of American reverence for Abraham Lincoln whose moving words are inscribed on the imposing façade of the Memorial: "With malice toward none, with charity for all."

KNOB CREEK FARM

"My earliest recollection was of the Knob Creek place . . . Our farm was composed of three fields. It lay in the valley surrounded by high hills and deep gorges." So wrote Abraham Lincoln in 1860 when invited to visit his native state.

On a paved highway two miles south of Hodgenville, the second traditional Lincoln cabin stands on rolling land at the site of the old Knob Creek homestead. In 1932 this replica of the Lincoln cabin was rebuilt with logs taken from the old log cabin of Austin Gollaher, a boyhood companion and schoolmate of young Abe Lincoln, who once rescued Abe from drowning in the swollen Knob Creek.

Surrounded by a split-rail fence, this replica of the boyhood home of Abe Lincoln is traditional in appearance and furnishings. A clay and stone chimney, a peg-hinged door and a small window are the only elaborations of the single-room cabin. Inside, the stone fireplace, hung with guns and cluttered with iron spider-skillets and kettles, cooked the food and warmed the small room and the half-loft which was reached by wall pegs. A stout bed, hovering over a trundle bed, a loom, a corner cabinet, crude tables and chairs, and a wooden churn filled the room. All the wood was hand-

Pigeon Creek Cabin Site, Abraham Lincoln and Nancy Hanks
Lincoln State Memorial, *Lincoln City, Indiana*

rived, from the puncheon floors to the rough shingles.

In later years Abraham Lincoln recalled many childhood memories of Knob Creek from 1811 to 1816: the chores of carrying water from the creek and gathering firewood from the hills, the large tree that sheltered the growing lad, a stone house on his route for carrying corn to Hodgen's Mill, his mother's lovely face as she sat by the fire and read her Bible to him, the baby brother who was born there and was buried on a hill near the cabin, the creek where he fished, and the vales where he gathered berries. Abe remembered planting seed in alternate hills and rows while the oldsters planted corn, only to have a big rain wash the seeds and corn away. Church meetings, corn shuckings, and logrollings interested the lad more than hunting and trapping. Young Abe and his sister Sarah helped and comforted frail Nancy Hanks Lincoln when Thomas Lincoln was away hunting and trapping or seeing what folk "were doing in faraway places."

The 230 acres of hills and bottom lands were fairly fertile and afforded a meager living for the Lincoln family. When Thomas Lincoln could spare Sarah and Abe from their chores, their more sensitive mother sent them two miles away to learn about books at the log schoolhouse. In scattered days at the "blab" schools they learned some of the fundamentals of the three R's from transient masters who judged the quality of studying by the volume of noise. At Mrs. Hodgen's free school, Abe thought it a waste of time to get sense from figures, but he did prefer "to know how to spell turkey than to be able to shoot its head off with a gun."

By experience Abe Lincoln learned much. Daily he tapped raw nature's secrets. From the Bible, the family's treasured Book, young Abe acquired a familiarity with the Scriptures which flavored his later speeches and writings. From travelers along the nearby roads he heard of folk and lore. Among pioneers he learned about hardships and hopes, the "short and simple annals of the poor."

Prodded by the flimsy hopes of the restless Thomas Lincoln, the Lincoln family left the Knob Creek farm for "promising" Indiana in the late fall of 1816. Abe Lincoln, an overgrown lad of seven, assisted his parents in packing their meager belongings and in ferrying them across the big Ohio River.

Kentucky Panel, Abraham Lincoln and Nancy Hanks
Lincoln State Memorial, *Lincoln City, Indiana*

PIGEON CREEK CABIN SITE

NANCY HANKS LINCOLN STATE MEMORIAL

Abe Lincoln's marks on southern Indiana have been admirably commemorated with state markers, trails, monuments and parks. This historic Lincolnland not only features Lincoln lore, but often provides recreational facilities too. From the flatboat landing near Rockport, a network of paved highways cross the land where Lincoln lived and worked. Lincoln State Park, which offers natural recreational facilities in a historic setting, adjoins the Nancy Hanks Lincoln State Memorial, which commemorates the pioneer mother and her illustrious son.

The imposing shrine, dedicated in 1943, is the outstanding feature of the Memorial. Built of Hoosier limestone and sandstone, the Abraham Lincoln Hall stands opposite the Nancy Hanks Hall, and an impressive semi-circle of cloisters and wall panels connects the two buildings. The five sculptured panels frame a heroic Lincoln in characteristic settings: the Kentucky Panel, featuring Abe's childhood years; the Indiana Panel, depicting his boyhood days; the Illinois Panel, indicating Lincoln's political ascendancy; the Washington Panel, featuring President Lincoln's years in command; and the Apotheosis —"And now he belongs to the ages."

A sloping alley connects these memorial buildings with the hillside grave of Nancy Hanks, and beyond the grave in the dense woods lies the preserved site of the Lincoln log cabin where Nancy Hanks Lincoln died on October 5, 1818. Bordered with a stout iron fence, the grave of the mother of President Lincoln is marked by a simple monument of Italian marble which was "erected by a friend of her martyred son, 1879."

Near by, a neat retaining wall encloses and protects the site of the Lincoln log cabin, built at Pigeon Creek in 1817. A unique monument of black sills and hearthstones, uncovered and re-set in 1934, marks the hallowed ground. In profound tribute, the inscribed marker admirably phrases its memorial thought: "As the altar of his home . . . this is the hearth set here to mark the place where Lincoln at his mother's knee learned that integrity and strength, that kindlinesss and love

Pigeon Creek Cabin, Lincoln Pioneer Village, *Rockport, Indiana*

of all beauty . . . have made the memory of his life and work a priceless heritage to all the world."

The extensive Nancy Hanks Lincoln Memorial is a far cry from the rugged homestead of 160 wooded acres the Lincolns knew. In 1816 they ferried across the Ohio and became the first pioneers to claim a squatter's tract on Pigeon Creek and dent a clearing there. Enduring a "half-faced log and bough camp" during that severe winter, the isolated family drank melted snow and lived on wild game and fish, using the animal furs for warmth.

With the thaws, young Abe, now strong and tall, toted pails of water from the spring and helped his father split logs to build a new cabin. They cleared seventeen acres of trees for fields of corn, wheat, and oats. In the forest Abe and Sarah plucked wild berries and nuts and located bee trees. By smoking out the bees and whacking down the trees, the family added honey to the scanty larder.

That fall, at the age of thirty-five Nancy Hanks died of dreaded "milk-sick" from weed-poisoned milk, leaving her legacy of Christian living and blessed memory to her desolate family. Aided by his bereft children, Thomas Lincoln buried his "beautiful Nancy" in the forest radiant with autumn colors. With increasing hard times, the motherless family sank into neglect and want—its lowest ebb in many lean years of poverty, illiteracy, and isolation. In 1836 A. Lincoln composed a plaintive poem of those hard times:

> When first my father settled here,
>   'Twas then the frontier line;
> The panther's scream filled night with fear
>   And bears preyed on the swine.

PIGEON CREEK CABIN

Lincoln Pioneer Village

The composite Lincoln Pioneer Village, surrounded by a pole fence, is conveniently assembled in City Park at Rockport. Built in 1935-1937 under the direction of the Spencer County Historical Association and the Rockport Park Board, this

Pigeon Creek Cabin (interior), Lincoln Pioneer Village,
Rockport, Indiana

rustic village contains a museum of memorabilia, the traditional Lincoln cabin of Pigeon Creek, and fifteen other log structures. These reproductions of the once scattered log houses are all connected with Spencer County and the fourteen formative years during which Abe Lincoln lived in the region, from 1816 to 1830. The entire rustic village is an historic mark honoring Abe Lincoln on this green land.

A sturdy replica of the Lincoln family home is featured in the traditional village, some sixteen miles south of the true site at Lincoln City. The reproduction of the Pigeon Creek Baptist Church, the old schoolhouse with its bell and wishing well, the Jones store where Abe clerked for a while, the two-story log mansion of James Gentry who hired the youth to work on his farm and in his store, and the Josiah Crawford cabin where Abe and Sarah worked and where he read books, are all reminiscent of the growing giant's rugged years at Pigeon Creek.

In the unfinished cabin on Pigeon Creek, Nancy Hanks Lincoln died in the fall of 1818, leaving young Abe of nine years, his sister Sarah, and an older cousin, Dennis Hanks, to help Thomas Lincoln combat the wilderness. In 1819 Thomas Lincoln went back to Kentucky, and in a borrowed wagon fetched his second wife, Sarah Bush Lincoln, along with her three children and her few possessions to join his unkempt family. The stepmother's scanty dowery, her steady pluck, and her abiding faith fortified the Lincoln family.

There were hard times and long pulls at Pigeon Creek. While the Lincoln clan of eight camped outside, Mrs. Lincoln prodded Thomas and the boys into readying the bare cabin. Soon split logs were laid on the dirt floor, a window and a door were hung, and her effects set in place. Pegs on the cabin wall enabled the boys to climb up to the dark loft, and a lean-to was added for the girls. Of their Indiana years Dennis Hanks said, "We lived the same as Indians, 'ceptin' we took an interest in politics and religion."

By his work and study life gradually became less severe for the growing Abe with the black, unruly hair and penetrating eyes. Soon a giant of six feet and four inches, he matched his growth with labor and learning. Until he was past twenty-two he helped his family and hired out to split

Thomas Lincoln Cabin, Lincoln Log Cabin State Park,
Coles County, Illinois

rails, studying and reading all along. In 1827 he built a scow for ferrying and doing errands on the Ohio. Once two men passengers on the scow paid him fifty cents each for hurrying them to a steamer. He could "scarcely credit . . . that a poor boy had earned a dollar in less than a day." After working in Gentry's general store, he and Allen Gentry built a flatboat, loaded it with store produce, and floated it down the Ohio and the Mississippi to New Orleans. In spite of a pirates' attack at Cave-in-Rock, the trip of three months was a successful adventure. A variety of such experiences enriched Abe Lincoln's maturing years.

Work never ceased. Abe Lincoln said his father taught him to work but never taught him to love it. When plowing, Abe read at the end of each furrow while allowing his horse to "breathe." Work was his necessity; study was his yearning. In a copybook, in round smooth script, he composed a bit of boyish doggerel, the earliest known example of his handwriting:

> Abraham Lincoln, his hand and pen,
> He will be good but God knows when.

PIGEON CREEK CABIN

(Interior)

The interior of the Pigeon Creek Cabin, now restored at Rockport, Indiana, is a tribute to the humble environment of young Abe Lincoln and an achievement by the research committees. The details in the replica are picturesque and accurate. The mud-chinked log walls, the board floors, and the rustic ceiling are typical of the frontier. In and around the large, necessary fireplace, the iron crane supports pots and kettles, the mantel holds treasured trinkets, and the chairs and churn are set for warmth. The wax figure of young Abe with his books completes the rustic scene.

Abe Lincoln grew physically strong and mentally alert in the improved Pigeon Creek home, encouraged by his kind stepmother. She managed to get for him a few more weeks of sporadic training in "blab" schools under wandering masters who used the rod for discipline and teaching. At home by a

New Salem Log Cabin Village (general view),
New Salem, Illinois

flickering fire, Abe often scraped the ciphers from wooden boards to clear space for more. He walked miles to borrow and return books, among them, Weem's *Life of Washington, Robinson Crusoe, Pilgrim's Progress, Aesop's Fables,* Grimshaw's *History of the United States,* and the *Declaration of Independence* which he memorized. On the frontier where many folks chiefly valued good coonskins, Abe cherished his few books as priceless treasures.

The few social functions were the sort that combined work and play, such as cornhuskings, logrollings, "house raisings," hog-killings, and quilting bees. There was an occasional square dance at the log schoolhouse. With the family Abe often attended the Pigeon Creek Baptist Church which Abe and his father helped to build. Like the Lincoln homestead, the community's cabins were dotted on isolated farms and the church was often a rugged haven. In case of emergency or bad weather, the women and children stayed with neighbors while the men and boys kept a roaring fire in the fireplace at the church and slept in its loft.

The frugal financial resources of the Lincoln family were often low, never high. During eleven hard years debt hovered over the Lincoln homestead at Pigeon Creek. In 1827 Thomas Lincoln obtained clear title to his west eighty acres by final payment on the assessed $160 and waived claim to the encumbered east eighty acres. Three years later Thomas Lincoln, restless and discouraged amid the towering forests, sold the small Lincoln homestead for $125. In two hand-built wagons the intrepid Lincolns treked some two hundred miles to the open prairies of "promising" Illinois.

THOMAS LINCOLN CABIN

In Coles County, Illinois, the two-room cabin of Thomas and Sarah Bush Lincoln stands south of Charleston, in the Lincoln Log Cabin State Park. This rustic abode is the second and last home of the Lincoln clan in Illinois.

Though less formidable than the forests of Indiana, the Illinois prairies were not gentle to the wandering family. The Lincolns first settled near Decatur on the Sangamon River. There they built a cabin, broke grasslands, and planted fields.

New Salem Dam and Mill on the Sangamon River,
New Salem, Illinois

However, "chills and fever" raged and "the winter of the deep snow" ruined feed and killed stock. Discouraged, Thomas Lincoln prospected for the Lincolns' last move.

At twenty-one Abe Lincoln was legally entitled to his own earnings, but he performed necessary chores for his family, made a boat to use on the Sangamon, and split countless rails at home and for hire. "He splits rails like a giant till he gits men watching and then rests his ax and tells a tale," one employer said. For one neighbor he split three thousand rails! Once, when ice floes overturned his boat, he was housed with his boss for several weeks while his frozen feet healed.

Gradually, Abe Lincoln gained experience and broadened his activities. For Denton Offutt, who was a wandering merchant of New Salem and Springfield, Abe and his stepbrother floated a cargo down the Illinois River and on the Mississippi to New Orleans. After returning to St. Louis, Abe walked a hundred miles along prairie trails to rejoin his father and his family who by this time had moved to Coles County.

For the last time Abe helped the Lincolns to get settled on their new homestead. He split logs to build the new cabin. He worked at planting and fencing a field and generally assisted his "folks" in getting settled comfortably. Having been a dutiful and helpful son, Abe Lincoln at the age of twenty-two left his family on the farm and set out for New Salem to seek his fortune. Leaving many rustic marks on the land, the alert giant challenged the bustling frontier.

NEW SALEM LOG CABIN VILLAGE

One of the outstanding restorations depicting early American life is the New Salem Log Cabin Village in the New Salem State Park near Petersburg, Illinois. This picturesque hamlet faithfully lifts a page of history from the frontier environment in which Lincoln worked and studied for six years. Vast sums and endless research produced graphic reconstructions among which are the dam on the Sangamon River, the Miller-Kelso dog-run house, the Miller blacksmith shop, the Lincoln-Berry store, and the Rutledge Tavern.

Strangely enough, New Salem's brief history almost co-incides with Lincoln's sojourn here from 1831 to 1837. Then,

Miller-Kelso Residence and Miller's Blacksmith Shop,
New Salem, Illinois

while Lincoln grew in deed and in memory, New Salem decayed from neglect and competition. After the turn of the century many individuals and organizations worked toward the reconstruction of New Salem. In 1931 the state of Illinois made its first of many appropriations for permament improvements to New Salem Park. Authentic furnishings for homes and shops, including original furniture, utensils, and wares, help to re-create the village scene. Typical flower and vegetable gardens, surrounded by shrubs and trees, have been planted to revive the historic picture. Formerly it was a village of meager living; now it is an historic mecca for millions of visitors.

NEW SALEM DAM AND MILL

In the New Salem Log Cabin Village stands a replica of the sturdy little mill and dam on the Sangamon River. In 1829 James Rutledge and John Cameron, assisted by local farmers and their teams, spanned the river with huge wooden bins and filled them with rocks and logs. Beside the dam, the newly erected saw and grist mill drew trade from miles around. Having established their mill, Rutledge and Cameron planned and laid out the town of New Salem on the bluff overlooking the Sangamon River.

On his way to New Orleans with his employer's flatboat loaded with produce, Lincoln and his crew floated down the Sangamon River. When his boat stranded on the Rutledge-Cameron dam, Lincoln met the New Salem villagers for the first time. Assisted by the settlers, he expertly bored holes in the prow of the boat to get it over the dam and proceeded on his way. Later, in 1831, he arrived back in New Salem to find promises of work and hopes of betterment, calling himself "a piece of driftwood."

Miller-Kelso Residence (interior), New Salem, Illinois

MILLER-KELSO RESIDENCE

In the New Salem State Park the restored Miller-Kelso residence is unique as a double log cabin with a dog-run, or breezeway. It is an essential part of the old village scene and the lore connected with the frontier life and times of Abraham Lincoln.

Today's faithful restorations include dwellings and shops dotted along the one and only main street of old New Salem. Before the days of city planning and zoning, nature kindly assisted in the development of the town. The high, smooth bluff overlooking the Sangamon River Valley was covered with lush grasses and rooted with tall trees.

Anticipating that New Salem might become a thriving river town, new settlers rushed in, and by 1832 the booming hamlet with its cheap and steady transportation on the river had reached its peak. The future of the area seemed assured. Optimists overlooked the real fact that river traffic was uncertain competition for the growing internal improvements of the nation.

In 1832 Joshua Miller bought two lots and an adjoining tract of land from Rutledge and Cameron for the sum of $25. Miller, village blacksmith and wagon maker, and Jack Kelso, hunter, fisherman, and philosopher, erected a double log cabin and a blacksmith shop. They had married sisters and made common use of the inviting breezeway between the two large cabins. Though Miller and Kelso were both busy, their efforts were directed in different channels. Miller worked diligently at his smithing while Kelso was engaged in fishing, trapping, and reading in the surrounding woods. In order to supplement the uncertain income provided by her husband, Mrs. Kelso took in boarders. Among these was Abraham Lincoln.

MILLER-KELSO RESIDENCE

(*Interior*)

The interior of the Kelso Cabin is a likely restoration of many typical homes in New Salem. The detail and accuracy of these furnishings create an interesting atmosphere for the curious traveler and the student of history. The beds with

Miller's Blacksmith Shop (interior), New Salem, Illinois

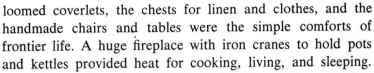

loomed coverlets, the chests for linen and clothes, and the handmade chairs and tables were the simple comforts of frontier life. A huge fireplace with iron cranes to hold pots and kettles provided heat for cooking, living, and sleeping.

This rustic, but kind environment did much to stabilize Lincoln and route him into constructive channels of learning and self-improvement. Becoming a friend of Jack Kelso and boarding in the Kelso home gave Lincoln the guidance of an informed friend and the home life that he needed. Lincoln slept in "makeshifts," but enjoyed the large fireplace room with the family.

While Lincoln worked as a store clerk and did odd chores, he also read and talked in his spare time. He borrowed Jack Kelso's books of Shakespeare and Burns and other classics and studied them, often memorizing passages and reciting them to his host. Once he walked eight miles to borrow a grammar from John Vance. Lincoln frequently asked Jack Kelso, Mentor Graham, and other readers to hold the books for checking his memory work and his answers to selected exercises.

These excursions into the classics, his groping for learning, and his knowledge of the Bible were gradually fused into Lincoln's thinking, talking, and writing. Truly, as Abe Lincoln said, "I will prepare myself and my time will come."

MILLER'S BLACKSMITH SHOP

(*Interior*)

The restored blacksmith shop of Joshua Miller stands beside the Miller-Kelso cabin in the New Salem State Park. The village smithy with its assortment of tools and gadgets once attracted many customers, but today it is viewed only by curious visitors. The strange tools for making hardware, welding irons, forging iron parts for wagons, and doing all sorts of repairs are collected in accurate detail.

This workshop was one of the busiest places in New Salem. From morning till night, Miller's fire roared as it was fanned by the big bellows and his anvil clanged as he forged hot irons into horseshoes, welded farm tools, and fashioned household implements.

First Lincoln-Berry Store (now the Post Office),
New Salem, Illinois

Abe Lincoln with his flair for odd tasks and honest money, his easy conversation, his droll tales, and his friendly manner often dropped into the blacksmith shop to work and chat with Miller and his customers. His powerful arms grappled with the chore while his keen wit was sharpened with this sociable usage.

As usual, in the summer of 1833, Abe Lincoln was looking for a job to help pay his growing debts and to supply his meager needs. Having just returned from his four months of enlistment in the Black Hawk War, Captain Lincoln had rare tales to relate about his regiment of home-town recruits, but he had no income and few prospects. He considered becoming a blacksmith, but really preferred lighter work in order to read and study law. A general store offered better chances to meet people and to improve himself. However, after he became involved in the Lincoln-Berry store he still often loitered at Miller's blacksmith shop, relating droll tales about his many experiences on the rivers and in the war and gathering tidbits of town talk.

FIRST LINCOLN-BERRY STORE

To the casual visitor entering restored New Salem, the replica of the first Lincoln-Berry store is the center of interest. For this single-room log cabin now houses the United States post office where uniquely stamped letters and cards may be mailed.

Rarely do any variations, such as the present post office, appear in the restoration of the village. The exterior of the old cabin is faithfully reconstructed, but now the interior is entirely devoted to present-day postal service. With three other stores, including the second Lincoln-Berry store, restored and equipped, the village restoration committees considered it advisable to use the first Lincoln-Berry store as a post office. This is entirely fitting, for Abe Lincoln began his service as postmaster of New Salem in his first store.

Although Lincoln had clerked in several other stores, this replica re-creates the setting of his first venture in business. In 1831 the Herndon brothers built this store and later sold it to Lincoln and William Berry. From two earlier postmasters

Second Lincoln-Berry Store, New Salem, Illinois

Lincoln took over the post office for a pittance and learned postal work by doing it. Thus he served as both a storekeeper and postmaster, netting very little money, but gaining valuable experience. During two years Lincoln and Berry plodded along with the general store, and then moved the stock and the post office to another location across the main street.

SECOND LINCOLN-BERRY STORE

The restorations of shops and dwellings in the New Salem State Park are now essentially finished. Excavations often uncovered old foundations, bits of china, ironwork, and various clues for the historic project. The last Lincoln-Berry store, being a focal point, was one of the first completed replicas, in both exterior and interior, of Lincoln's former haunts. The second and better-known Lincoln-Berry store was New Salem's only sheathed building and it is expertly restored with crude boarded walls and rived shingles.

This sheathed structure represented many hopes and more hardships. Several men managed or mismanaged the business before Lincoln and Berry bought the store in 1833 and moved their stock and the post office from across the street into it. For a while the combined stock drew more customers, but the connection soon proved unfavorable and Lincoln gave up the post office and sold his interest in the store to Berry.

During the span of its shifting ownerships, the old store building served many people, notably Abraham Lincoln himself. Here in the boarded lean-to which was used as a storeroom he often studied or slept. This replica, like many others in the village is not only a tribute to Abe Lincoln, but it also graphically portrays the modes and methods of life on an American frontier.

SECOND LINCOLN-BERRY STORE

(*Interior*)

The authentic details in the furnishings of the interiors in the New Salem State Park are impressive and varied. Several general stores exhibit wares, necessities, and luxuries which

Second Lincoln-Berry Store (interior), New Salem, Illinois

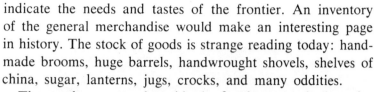

indicate the needs and tastes of the frontier. An inventory of the general merchandise would make an interesting page in history. The stock of goods is strange reading today: handmade brooms, huge barrels, handwrought shovels, shelves of china, sugar, lanterns, jugs, crocks, and many oddities.

The sturdy counter alongside the fireplace was the bargaining center of the large room. Under it the valuable wares were hidden, and over it prices were haggled and hard money and good produce exchanged. Under such a counter, Postmaster Lincoln kept the incoming and outgoing mail in separate boxes and placed the postage money in a sock. All postage on letters and newspapers was estimated by weight and distance and paid by the receiver when the mail arrived at its destination. Lincoln kept the postal receipts in this "safe" sock till he was ready to make his reports and deduct his portion. From this counter Lincoln often took mail to his friends, carrying it in the crown of his hat. This unique method of carrying valuables continued into his later walks in life.

The contacts with people, the varied experiences as postmaster and storekeeper, and the frequent lulls for study and reading afforded Lincoln more benefits than the material income indicated.

RUTLEDGE TAVERN

The name of Rutledge appears often in the history of New Salem and in the restoration of the New Salem State Park. The Rutledge Tavern is today a replica of the old Rutledge home after it was converted into a combined home and boarding place. In 1828, after James Rutledge and his nephew,.John Cameron, built the mill and laid out the town site, Rutledge built a large two-room cabin for his growing family. As immigrants came to the Sangamon Valley and the town boomed, Rutledge added two frame rooms to accommodate paying guests. In the old town the Rutledge Tavern was the first to be built and the last to succumb, falling to the ground in 1880.

The tavern was quite an establishment in its day. The rail fences, the dugout, the barns and several bins were clustered around the sturdy house. The ash hopper, an essential part

Rutledge Tavern, New Salem, Illinois

of every household, was the receptacle for dead ashes to produce lye drip for making soap.

The tavern had an interesting history and many occupants. The large east room was probably the combined kitchen, dining room, and guest-sitting room. The west room accommodated the family and an occasional lady guest. The two lean-to rooms were used for family bedrooms and storage. The loft, or half-story, served as a large bedroom for the men and boys. When Lincoln first came to New Salem, he boarded at the tavern and slept in the loft with the other men guests. He frequented the "common room" where townspeople and travelers gathered for food and gossip.

RUTLEDGE TAVERN

(Interior)

Legend and lore demanded a true reproduction of the Rutledge Tavern and its rustic interior in New Salem State Park. Old newspapers, diaries, and letters have contributed many accurate details. Puncheon floors, spotted with hand-loomed rugs, were the mode of the day. Heavy beams held the ceiling logs. All the walls were firmly chinked with mud and clay.

The twin chimneys at either end of the tavern were massive and serviceable. The large east room had an extension dining table in the center and many items of comfort and pleasure made it an inviting place. The substantial chairs and chests and the spinning wheel indicated good living. Banter, wit, and tall tales were heard around the fireplace. Lincoln, whose physical prowess tamed the wild Clary gang, was also appreciated as clever with tales and jokes. This rail-splitting giant was a regular member of the New Salem debating society, and the subjects used by the debating teams were often rehearsed in the tavern.

The tavern afforded a meeting place for the people of the town. The Rutledge family was busy, gracious and hospitable to strangers. Ann Rutledge, the pretty daughter, was the pride of the community and a favorite in the tavern. Although she was betrothed to a distant swain, Lincoln admired her deeply. After the Rutledges moved to a farm north of the village,

Rutledge Tavern (interior), New Salem, Illinois

Lincoln often visited them on his surveying trips. When Ann died of "fever" in 1835, her death saddened the community and Abe Lincoln.

VANDALIA COURTHOUSE

Formerly the Vandalia Courthouse, this restored memorial was once the wilderness capitol of the state, the third Statehouse of Illinois. The solid building had a turbulent history as a capitol and later as the courthouse in its community. Now this old structure of varied services is preserved as a state memorial.

In 1834 Abraham Lincoln of New Salem, novice lawmaker from Sangamon County, first saw Vandalia from a jostling stagecoach whose driver dramatically blew his horn to announce the end of the seventy-five mile journey of thirty-six tiresome hours over muddy roads. Having been elected a member of the lower house, Lincoln had borrowed $200 from a friend to launch his political career. This country lawyer, who usually wore homespun clothes, was wearing a $60 tailor-made suit.

By work and integrity Lincoln forged ahead. He became floor leader of the Whigs, a leading political party. Soon he was accepted as an esteemed member of the Long Nine, a group of politicians who were tall of stature and long in influence. Local, state, and national issues were debated and passed or rejected in this Statehouse. The national bank, public improvements, the relief of the Panic of 1837, and sundry other issues were the hue and cry of many prominent leaders in and out of Illinois. Lincoln was meeting the great and the near great and rapidly becoming one of them.

As a trusted member of the Long Nine, Lincoln helped to move the capitol to Springfield. "As Vandalia the victim waned, Springfield the victor waxed." Lincoln, a struggling country lawyer, rode on the crest of politics both in the old and new capitols of his adopted state. Success was finally abetting his long and laborious climb from nothing to something. At last he was a qualified lawyer and a power in state politics.

In 1839, after the capitol was located in Springfield, the state conveyed the old Statehouse to Vandalia and its county.

*Vandalia Courthouse (former Illinois State Capitol),
Vandalia, Illinois*

Two decades later the building was decaying and only the outer shell of brick stood. In 1919 the state of Illinois purchased the grounds and building for $60,000 to preserve them as an historic memorial.

SANGAMON COUNTY COURTHOUSE

More than a century ago the present Sangamon County Courthouse was proudly erected as the new Illinois State Capitol at Springfield, and has been in constant service during many kaleidoscopic changes ever since. The yellow stone building of Greek-revival style was centered in a town square when Springfield had but 2,500 scattered inhabitants. Now it is the Sangamon County Courthouse in a bustling metropolis. By wit and strategy the Whigs, lead by Lincoln and the Long Nine, had championed Springfield as a more central location, while Stephen A. Douglas and the Democrats had defended the losing Vandalia for the coveted site. According to an act suggested by Representative Lincoln, "no less than $50,000 and two acres of land" had to be donated by the city chosen for the capitol site. At a huge bonfire rally around the whipping post on the public square, the citizens of Springfield quickly pledged the money and land conditional to the relocation of the capitol.

On July 4, 1837, the cornerstone of the state's fourth capitol building was laid at Springfield. In 1853, after many delays, the classic stone structure was completed at a total cost of $260,000, twice the original estimate. Centered in the three-acre square and constructed of stone from a local quarry, the majestic building was considered an architectural wonder of the state. After the present larger state capitol was finally completed in 1888, the old capitol was sold to Sangamon County for a courthouse. Many alterations have been made in the old building, but the most remarkable innovation was the raising of the entire structure and the building under it of a new ground floor. This century-old edifice represents an historic mark of Lincoln on our land.

Sprawling, expanding Springfield had a maturing effect on the growing political acumen of Abe Lincoln. Taking leave of his constituents in New Salem on April 15, 1837, Lincoln rode horseback into Springfield with all his belongings in his

Sangamon County Courthouse (former Illinois State Capitol),
Springfield, Illinois

saddlebags. He accepted free lodging above a store kept by Joshua F. Speed, who soon became a trusted friend. On the same day the *Springfield Journal* stated: "J. T. Stuart and A. Lincoln, Attorneys and Counsellors at Law, will practice conjointly, in the courts of this Judicial District." Lincoln had slowly advanced along his rustic road to fame from his duties as a legislator in Vandalia to the time of his many services in Springfield.

In the growing town where he planned to make his home, Lincoln was lonely but respected. Wagons laden with state archives had plodded from Vandalia to Springfield in a heavy rain. State officials moved into Springfield helping to make it the political, judicial, and social center of the state. In June of 1838 Lincoln was elected a trustee of the new capital city. He served in this capacity till the following year, when he was instrumental in obtaining from the state legislature a new charter for his adopted city.

By the fall of 1840 the fourth state capitol building was nearly completed and was proudly in use for legislative sessions during the bitter struggles between the Whigs and Democrats over the pressing issues of banking, state debts, internal improvements, panic and hard times, and slavery. Lincoln, who was recovering from an illness, attempted with his colleagues to prevent the Democrats from packing the state Supreme Court by increasing the number of justices from four to nine. But the packing measure passed, and Stephen A. Douglas became one of the new appointees on the Supreme Court bench.

The old fourth Statehouse is rich in Lincoln associations. After completing his fourth term as a legislator in Illinois, lawyer Lincoln argued cases before the Supreme Court in this edifice and made frequent use of the state and Federal court libraries. These experiences contributed to his election as Congressman of the United States. In this same Statehouse Lincoln first took public issue with Douglas. Here he made his famous "house divided against itself" speech, which so dramatically stated his view that slavery was unjust and unsound. Here were his headquarters during his 1860 campaign for the Presidency. Finally, here his remains rested on May 4, 1865, before the burial at Oak Ridge Cemetery in Springfield.

The Governor's Mansion, Springfield, Illinois

THE GOVERNOR'S MANSION

Springfield

Since 1856 this stately old executive mansion has been the official home of the governors of Illinois. The imposing white brick structure stands on a beautifully landscaped knoll on Jackson Street, between Fourth and Fifth Streets. This century-old edifice has been repaired and redecorated, but it remains structurally the same as when it was first occupied. It is still a haven for the governor and his family, a mecca for politicians, and a point of pride with residents of Springfield.

Abraham Lincoln crossed the threshold of fame when he frequented the home of the governors of his adopted state. From the time the capitol was moved to Springfield in 1839 till the present mansion was built in 1856, the governors lived in a dwelling on the northwest corner of Eighth Street and Capitol Avenue (then Market Street). Lincoln, as a Representative and as a lawyer, frequently visited the homes and offices of the state's executives.

Before entering this national role, Abraham Lincoln and several other prominent figures in statecraft helped to direct and enforce the administrative affairs of the governors. Acting-Governor Wood and the Lincoln group gave political and social service to the ailing executive and his state. The governor's office in the mansion, as well as those in the Statehouse, were generously placed at the disposal of Lincoln before and during his candidacy for the Presidency in 1860. Abe Lincoln never "ran" for the Presidency, he modestly "walked" for it. During his strategy of silence, Lincoln's campaign managers and friends circulated his well-known views on the current problems and praised his personal attributes. Since his political and personal characteristics were known from earlier, more vocal campaigns, Lincoln discreetly "walked" daily from his home to his headquarters in the governor's mansion, to his offices in the Statehouse, and to the Lincoln-Herndon law office. He did many chores at home while the managers of the Republican Party worked the field.

Social affairs at the governor's mansion have always been attended by all the elite of the capital. Here the Lincoln fam-

Old Main Building, Knox College, Galesburg, Illinois

ily often visited the governor's family and mingled with the crowds for informal visits or formal balls and receptions. Abraham Lincoln, wearing ill-fitting clothes on his giant frame, but always using his banter and wit along with his penetrating powers of observation, was a unique and wholesome personage in the changing scene of his day.

For a century the stately home of the governors of Illinois has been the setting of many historic and colorful events, but it is the Lincoln legend that glorifies the entire panorama.

OLD MAIN BUILDING

Galesburg

At Knox College in Galesburg, Illinois, stands Old Main Building, the only structure extant that is directly associated with the Lincoln-Douglas Debates of 1858. A plaque commemorating one of the famous debates for the seat of United States Senator from Illinois is now located near the front entrance of Old Main.

> This memorial tablet is placed here
> to recall the joint debate between
> ABRAHAM LINCOLN and STEPHEN A. DOUGLAS,
> whose words these walls echoed
> October the 7th 1858.

"Equality among the different states is a cardinal principle upon which all our institutions rest."

DOUGLAS.

"He is blowing out the moral lights around us who contends that whoever wants slaves has a right to hold them."

LINCOLN.

Knox College, proudly attesting its connections with a notable mark of Lincoln on the state of Illinois, has made long and useful progress in educational channels. Planted on fertile soil, the pioneer college was chartered by a reluctant Illinois legislature under pressure from Representative Lincoln at Vandalia in 1837. Known as Knox Manual Labor College, it opened its doors to male students in 1841. The original plan to train young men to preach the gospel has been expanded to provide broad educational programs. The name has been simplified to Knox College, and women are now admitted. However, the primary tradition of "working a way through college" still prevails.

Old Main, carefully restored through the efforts of Janet Greig Post, has become a national monument because Abraham Lincoln once stood at its front entrance to debate with Stephen A. Douglas. There the two rivals marshaled their best stratagems and addressed the largest crowd in the memorable series of seven debates across the state of Illinois. Later, Knox College bestowed upon Abraham Lincoln his only honorary degree.

During the summer and fall of 1858 the race for a place in the United States Senate between Democratic Senator Douglas and the Republican aspirant, Lincoln, set the Illinois prairies ablaze with rallies and crowds. Senator Douglas was the seasoned standard-bearer for the strong Democratic Party. Abraham Lincoln, having tasted of Washington politics during his illuminating but uneventful Congressional term for the limping Whig Party, from 1847 to 1849, sought to dig deep into national problems and to re-enter the challenging political scene under the banner of the new Republican Party.

The seven scheduled debates, with personal appearances crammed in between, afforded many gala occasions. Thousands of persons—town residents on special trains and country folk by ox-wagons, buggies, or on horseback—flocked to crowded areas, crossroads, and festive gatherings to witness the battle of words for the senatorship. Usually, Senator Douglas, accompanied by his wife, several secretaries, and some political henchmen, traveled in a gaily decorated private car. On the same train a festooned flat car carried a cannon which was fired by two uniformed men to boom to the prairie folk the approach of Little Giant Douglas. Frequently, Lincoln rode a horse to convenient points, and sometimes he traveled as an ordinary passenger on the same train that pulled the Senator's two cars. The candidates respected each other's political acumen, but Douglas in angry outbursts denounced Lincoln as a "wretch" or a "sneak." In restraint Lincoln retorted with "fraud" and "falsehood." Significantly, each adversary had his own shorthand reporter to keep the record straight.

The debates were highly publicized and the speeches were read not only in Illinois, but all over the nation. As spokesman for the new Republican Party—which had been organized in 1854 in Ripon, Wisconsin, by a group of Northern Democrats, Whigs, and Free-Soilers—Abraham Lincoln denounced slavery as wrong and dividing the nation. As a leader for the Democratic Party, Senator Douglas argued for legality and constitutionality. The spectacular campaigns were waged with banners, parades, fireworks, and pageantry. Lincoln and Douglas had already spoken in Chicago and they followed a fixed schedule to debate in seven towns—Ottawa, Freeport, Jonesboro, Charleston, Galesburg, Quincy, and Alton. Between the seven points, each candidate spoke almost daily during four months to crowds at outdoor rallies and in packed halls.

At Ottawa a crowd of 10,000 heard Lincoln and Douglas argue under a blazing sun. In Freeport some 15,000 were soothed by the soaring oratory of Douglas who was verbosely evasive to Lincoln's realistic questions. These questions were the core of much of Lincoln's logic and became known as the Freeport Doctrine: Can a territory legislate slavery in or out if Congress cannot? Is a territory more powerful than the Congress which created it? Can water rise above its source? At Charleston a parade of festooned wagons and spangled horsemen honored Abe Lincoln who fenced with Douglas and visited with Thomas and Sarah Bush Lincoln and many friends.

On October 7, 1858, at Galesburg, a strong wind whipped the street decorations. In pageantry Lincoln was featured as the champion of "Freedom" and Douglas was shown riding for a fall as he tried to straddle two horses, "Dred Scott" and "Popular Sovereignty." The rivals spoke to immense crowds which had braved the weather and gathered on the campus of Knox College. Across the entire front of Old Main Building was stretched a large banner, "Knox College for Lincoln," a symbol of appreciation for his services in chartering the college and of approbation for his moral conviction that slavery was a wrong. In this fifth debate under the pounding of

Lincoln-Douglas Debate Memorial, Washington Park, Quincy, Illinois

Douglas, Abraham Lincoln clearly formulated his arguments and became a convincing spokesman for the Republican Party.

LINCOLN-DOUGLAS DEBATE MEMORIAL

Quincy

Like a huge page of great history, unfolded for the world to see and ponder, this unique granite and bronze plaque in the heart of Quincy, Illinois, is a picturesque memorial of the sixth stirring debate between Abraham Lincoln and Stephen A. Douglas. This graphic plaque of heroic size recalls one of the seven far-reaching debates between Lincoln, the challenger, and Douglas, who was defending his position for re-election as United States Senator from Illinois. It is a vivid mark of Lincoln on our land, faithful in its interpretation and rare in its artistic form.

This memorial to the Lincoln-Douglas debate of October 13, 1858, is a permanent structure that stirs pride and interest in thousands of patriotic Americans. Many years after the famous debate, the members of the Exchange Club of Quincy requested that the state of Illinois make an appropriation for a suitable marker. Forthwith some $10,000 was allocated and the eminent Lorado Taft was commissioned to design and execute the memorial. On October 13, 1936, the Lincoln-Douglas Memorial was dedicated before a proud audience, on the exact site where the earnest debaters,' seventy-eight years earlier, had addressed a throng of approximately fifteen thousand.

Today the Lorado Taft masterpiece commemorates Lincoln and Douglas and their times. The relief is of bronze, with a green patina, mounted on a block of granite. The plaque depicts a typical lecture platform of the last century. Lincoln, tall and strong, and Douglas, short and stout, are faithfully portrayed, and the costumed figures and the tall trees in the background set the scene of a bygone era. Lincoln, a veritable giant, hurled questions that made the Little Giant Douglas flinch and caused the audience to ponder the grave questions of slavery, state sovereignty, and constitutionality. At Quincy Douglas spoke for an hour. Then Lincoln talked for an hour and a half, and Douglas had a final rebuttal of thirty minutes.

Saint-Gaudens' Statue of Abraham Lincoln, Lincoln Park,
Chicago, Illinois

In the battle of giants many strong words were flung at the contemporary issues.

At Quincy, during the sixth debate, Lincoln projected the cause of the Republican Party against slavery and a "house divided," and he accused the Democratic Party of not taking into account the rights and wrongs of slavery. While pointing out the basic differences in the two parties, Lincoln much impressed Carl Schurz who had been sent from Wisconsin to Illinois by the Republican central committee to make speeches in Lincoln's behalf. Observing the contrasts in the two rivals, Schurz realized that Lincoln's high-pitched voice, his awkward mannerisms, and his powerful logic towered over Douglas' worn voice, his natty attire, and his belligerent orations.

From the fiery debate platforms in the towns and hamlets of Illinois Abraham Lincoln's plausible words were spoken not merely to the local audiences, but also to the thinking people of the nation. Lincoln lost the Senate race to Douglas, but two years later Lincoln won the Presidency, largely because of his national reputation gained in these sensational debates in Illinois. Lincoln emerged from the bogs of obscurity in Illinois to the threshold of fame in Washington, D. C. The many words of Little Giant Douglas carried his day. The wisdom of the Great Giant, Lincoln, has echoed for a century.

SAINT-GAUDENS' STATUE OF LINCOLN

Chicago

Standing majestically in Lincoln Park, in Chicago, is the famous statue of Abraham Lincoln which for sixty years has been another great mark of Lincoln on our land. This bronze giant was the gift of Eli Bates and was designed and executed by Augustus Saint-Gaudens. In 1865 Lake Park was renamed Lincoln Park to honor the late President, and philanthropist Bates felt that a statue of Lincoln must occupy a commanding position in the open park, "far from the madding crowd of life's ignoble strife." Among his final benefactions in 1881, Eli Bates bequeathed $25,000 for a fountain in Lincoln Park and $40,000 for the erection of a noble statue of Lincoln.

The Bates trustees were wise in commissioning the versatile Saint-Gaudens to make both the statue and the fountain. Relying on his genius, fidelity and skill, they made no restrictions on design or time. The work of Saint-Gaudens on the Lincoln memorial is a great story. The talented sculptor was impressed with the vastness of the Lincoln country and the naïveté of its people. Studying Lincoln's life and habits, Saint-Gaudens and his helpers worked in a century-old barn on both a standing and a seated portrait of Lincoln. They used "Lincoln-shaped" men for models and an original life mask of Lincoln. The rustic park site was enhanced by Stanford White who designed the huge pedestal for the statue and the long, semicircular bench and bases. The bases bear written excerpts, cast in bronze, from Lincoln's Gettysburg Address, his Second Inaugural Address, and his Cooper Institute Speech.

On a dreary Sunday, October 22, 1887, the Lincoln statue was unveiled. Leonard Swett, who for eleven years had ridden the eighth Judicial District with Lincoln, made the official address. He related personal stories about the self-reliant Lincoln who "bridged back" from middle age to youth and learned to spell well. He said that the Declaration of Independence was Lincoln's "perfect standard of political truth" and that he believed in God as the Supreme Ruler of the world and in himself as "an instrument and leader in forces of freedom." As Lincoln's fifteen-year-old grandson pulled the cord that loosened the flag from the pensive bronze giant, the sun struggled through the clouds and shone on a hushed, tearful audience. The standing Lincoln inspired them.

Since that day throngs from all over the nation and the world have stood in awe before the heroic Lincoln, revering the bronze giant that is a great work of art. This masterpiece of metal and stone is the product of honor and eminence achieved by three men: Lincoln, the frontiersman rising to speak to his people; Saint-Gaudens, talented son of the melting pot of New York; Eli Bates, grateful cripple and benefactor. Their triumphs over adversity and handicap, their ambitious devotion to cause and country, and their achievements in varied and useful service are inspiring stories of noble living in the American way.

The Saint-Gaudens statue shows Lincoln standing in deep contemplation, having risen from his chair to speak to the people whom he loved and served. After his election to the

United States Congress in 1847, Lincoln made his first political address in fast-growing Chicago. As a corporation lawyer, he had often made court pleas and speeches there. In 1854 he left his home in Springfield and journeyed over Illinois to talk in behalf of the opponents of the Kansas-Nebraska Bill which Stephen A. Douglas had introduced. Douglas, a Democrat, was opposed by many minor parties such as Free-Soilers, Abolitionists, Know-Nothings, as well as by the Whigs, and all these by 1856 were fused into a new Republican Party. During these spirited and confused times, Lincoln became prominently identified with the new party. His views were well-known in 1858 when he entered as a Republican into the Senate race against Senator Douglas. His early address brought enthusiastic support in Chicago. The Lincoln-Douglas debates at seven points across Illinois were publicized and read in Chicago. Though Senator Douglas was re-elected, Lincoln had become a national figure.

With astute awareness of the conflicts between the leaders of the Republican Party for the Presidential nomination in 1860, Abraham Lincoln, lawyer and spokesman for the frontier, accepted numerous invitations to speak in strategic centers in the East. His ungainly appearance belied his logic and force. His grandeur of thought and his simplicity of expression received favorable press reports from leading newspapers. In October of 1859, on the request of Henry Ward Beecher's church in Brooklyn, New York, and following an introduction by William Cullen Bryant, Abraham Lincoln delivered a carefully prepared oration to a packed hall at Cooper Institute. Horace Greeley praised Lincoln, saying that no other man had ever made such an impression in his first appeal to a New York audience. The Cooper Union speech put within Lincoln's grasp an excellent chance for the nomination for the Presidency.

In 1860 the Republican Nominating Convention in Chicago made national history. That noisy, colorful convention passed over many aspirants, notably William H. Seward of New York and Salmon P. Chase of Ohio, and named Lincoln as its standard bearer for the Presidency. On May 18, 1860, while twice as many swarmed outside, ten thousand people in the pine-board Wigwam witnessed demonstrations, pageantry, and

The Abraham Lincoln Home, Springfield, Illinois

balloting that nominated a frontier rail splitter for the Presidency. A delegation of notables left Chicago to notify Honest Abe, who had discreetly remained at home in Springfield.

The throngs who today pay tribute to the Saint-Gaudens statue of Lincoln recall that the contemplative giant, rising from a chair of state, had a long climb from obscurity to greatness. Nor was the chair of state an easy one. A patriot may well repeat Lincoln's famous words spoken at his Second Inauguration and inscribed on the outside of the massive exedra:

> With malice toward none, with charity for all, with firmness in the right, as God gives us to see the right, let us strive on . . .

THE ABRAHAM LINCOLN HOME

The Abraham Lincoln home in Springfield is an intensely personal memorial which is carefully maintained by the state of Illinois. Open daily except Thanksgiving, Christmas, and New Year's Day, this ante-bellum dwelling has attracted thousands of interested visitors since 1887, when Robert Todd Lincoln gave it to the state to be opened to the public free of charge.

The Abraham Lincoln home, the only house that Lincoln ever owned, stands today serenely on the corner of Eighth and Jackson Streets. Built in 1839 by the Reverend Charles Dresser on a corner lot of 50 by 152 feet, it was originally a cottage of one story and two attic rooms. In January of 1844, Abraham Lincoln purchased this property, for $1200 cash and a $300 equity he held in a downtown lot, from Reverend Dresser, the Episcopal minister who had married Lincoln and Mary Todd two years previously. Their first two years had been spent in boarding houses and at the Globe Tavern where board and room were $4 per week. To this desirable home Lincoln then brought his wife and infant son, Robert Todd, and crossed a threshold which for some sixteen years was destined to be the haven of his family and friends, a center of joy and tragedy, and the scene of his approach to fortune and fame.

The Lincoln house is the original structure, standing in the same location as when the Lincolns lived in it. Built entirely of wood, it is stoutly and appropriately constructed and decorated. The house is made of native woods. The framework and floors are oak, the laths are hand-split hickory, the doors, doorframes, and weatherboarding are black walnut. The original shingles were rived walnut. Many wooden pegs and some handmade nails were used in the construction. For many years the exterior was painted white, with green shutters, but now a tinted beige closely resembles the original coloring.

The Lincolns made some changes while they lived here. The low retaining wall and fence were built in 1850. Lincoln wrote a local brickmaker on June 11 of that year and ordered "brick of suitable quality and sufficient number . . . to build a front fence on a brick foundation." Five years later a similar fence was extended on the Jackson Street side, with a high board fence continuing to the carriage house. Needing room for her growing family, mindful of Lincoln's prosperity as a lawyer and his success as an officeholder, and venting her vanity and social aspirations, Mrs. Lincoln prodded Lincoln to make the house into the two full stories she felt were in keeping with their social position in Springfield. The story is told that while Lincoln was away on legal business, all Mrs. Lincoln's talents for luxuries and niceties were mustered for enlarging the structure. When Lincoln returned and approached his home, he inquired of a loitering urchin who lived in that fine home. The lad quickly replied, "Mrs. Lincoln and Mr. Lincoln and their boys."

Essentially reminiscent of the Lincolns, this dwelling has, however, been occupied by others. When Lincoln was in Congress and his family lived in and around Washington, he rented the Springfield home for $90 per year. Upon entering the Presidency, Lincoln leased his home to Lucian A. Tilton, head of the Great Western Railroad, for $350 per year. In 1883 Osburn H. Oldroyd rented the Lincoln house and used it as a museum for his extensive collection of Civil War and Lincoln mementoes. Robert Todd Lincoln gave the property to the state of Illinois and the deed was recorded on July 29, 1887. Oldroyd, as the first custodian, remained there till 1893, when he moved his collection to Washington, D. C., and later sold it to the Federal Government.

Lincoln's home was the scene of many activities. For Lincoln it was the center of an ever-widening circle, legal and political. As a prominent lawyer, Lincoln walked from his home to his law office, which he shared with William H. Herndon. His frequent visits to the governor's mansion, his forays into the courts at the Statehouse, his adventures into the circuit courts were invariably climaxed by his return to his beloved home. At his doorway he often greeted crowds of well-wishers during the campaign of 1860. Here he spoke warm farewells to many friends and citizens on his departure for Washington on February 11, 1861.

Today the Lincoln dwelling is a combined shrine and museum, a mecca for those who admire Lincolniana, and a vivid portrait of the last century to those interested in the living of yesteryears. Well-preserved and meticulously cared for, today the century-old Lincoln home serenely surveys the moving present and is nostalgically reminiscent of its own colorful past. Abraham Lincoln's historic home faithfully preserves an indelible mark of Lincoln on our land.

LINCOLN'S HOME

Entrance hall

The modest front entrance of the Lincoln home is a recessed stoop which frames the front door leading to the entrance hall. At this threshold many hands, from the humble to the great, have used the original doorbell which still announces guests to the Lincoln domain. The front hall is inviting and convenient, providing passage into the downstairs rooms and a simple walnut stairway to the rooms above.

One's immediate impression upon entering this ante-bellum home is both pleasing and poignant. Faithful reproductions and restorations commemorate and decorate the entire dwelling. In the hall and throughout the interior the original wallpaper has been carefully reproduced. The original hatrack and umbrella stand graces the front hall. Flanking the entrance hall are the double parlors, the dining room, and the family sitting room which are furnished and arranged much in the Lincoln mode. When the Lincolns went to Washington, D. C. in 1861, they sold their household furnishings, most of which were bought by the Lucian Tilton family who rented the house. The Tiltons took most of the furniture to Chicago in 1869 and lost it in the Great Fire of 1871. However, the Abraham Lincoln Association of Springfield has furnished the rooms on the first floor with some Lincoln pieces. Other relics have come from the homes of relatives and friends of Lincoln's time. Lincoln's shaving mirror, his favorite chair, Mrs. Lincoln's sewing rocker, and Tad's little chair are in the family living room. Their own table adorns the dining room.

Abraham and Mary Lincoln moved into their attractive home in 1844, when their eldest son, Robert Todd, was an infant. The other three Lincoln sons were born in this house: Edward Baker, "Eddie" (1846-1850); William Wallace, "Willie" (1850-1862); and Thomas, "Tad" (1853-1871). The first tragedy befell the Lincolns when Eddie died there. Baby Tad's lisping cajoled special favors from his doting father and the houseful of growing boys welded together this remarkable family.

Lincoln once wrote a friend, "My marrying is a matter of profound wonder." Truly his home life was blended joy and sadness, anxiety and peace, defeat and victory. He and his wife were opposites in every way. He was tall and thin; she was short and stout. He was slow and easy-going, while she was quick and volatile. He was humble and she was aristocratic. His personality and mind grew continuously. She remained in a fixed pattern. However, both were ambitious, determined and willing to make sacrifices, and they loved each other. Both had shortcomings. He was careless, often dowdy, and frequently abstracted. She was hard to please and easily angered.

Personal stories about the Lincoln family are legion. Lincoln was overindulgent and left the upbringing of the boys to "Mother," who was forbearing and too strict by turns. Lincoln loved to sprint with his boys up and down the stairway or to tussle with them on the floor—till reprimanded by "Mother" and sent into the yard. Lincoln milked his own cow, curried his horse, and cut and stacked his own firewood, often assisted by his "dear codgers." The cow was usually staked on a vacant lot nearby where the boys played and romped. Often Lincoln paused after doing the milking to romp with them, but upon

Lincoln's Home (entrance hall), Springfield, Illinois

hearing a sharp demand for milk for the next meal, Lincoln would run home with the full milk pail without spilling a drop, a skill he kept from his childhood chore of toting water from springs.

Up life's long hill Abraham Lincoln had "toted" many worries and reverses and had run with few joys and victories. The early privations and defeats in local and state politics were climaxed by his loss of the race against Senator Douglas in 1858. But his service as state legislator for four terms and his sojourn in Washington, D. C. as a congressman for two years built his political stature. Both the defeats and victories enlarged his horizon, expanded his views, and gained him many friends. With his family Lincoln could stoically meet the many defeats and serenely accept the few victories.

One late Saturday afternoon, on May 17, 1860, a group of thirty-five men with mixed emotions of doubt and concern approached the Lincoln home. On the recessed porch they met two lads, about seven and nine. The older boy, who was accosted by William M. Evarts, said he was Lincoln's son. The smaller lad chimed in, "I'm a Lincoln, too." The committee from the Republican Nominating Convention stood at the entrance laughing and ready for the ordeal—whether good or bad—of notifying Honest Abe Lincoln, frontiersman and rail splitter, of his nomination for the Presidency. Abraham Lincoln calmly met them at the door and graciously ushered them from the front hall into the north parlor of his comfortable home.

LINCOLN'S HOME

North parlor

The north parlor, the largest room in the Lincoln house, was adequate for formal entertaining. The long room, 36 by 15 feet, is cheered by a large fireplace centered on one long wall. Damask draperies like the originals adorn the windows. Carpets and rugs of floral designs are decorative and characteristic of the period. Sturdy chairs and a small sofa with black horsehair covering are placed against the papered walls. A glorified whatnot exhibiting bric-a-brac adorns one corner. Handsome French mirrors, obtained by Mrs. Lincoln, reflect

Lincoln's Home (north parlor), Springfield, Illinois

this pleasant and historic setting. During a hundred-year cycle the Lincolns' fashionable furnishings slowly became antiquated and finally became fashionable again, the antiques in our modern age.

Lincoln's Springfield home appears sumptuous compared with his log cabin years. His mind was so rich in varied experiences that his material wants were limited, but Mrs. Lincoln chose to live "in the manner born." Lincoln felt more at ease in the other rooms where he freely slouched in his stocking feet, but he often pleasantly visited and joked with his friends in the parlor. With ease and charm he assisted Mrs. Lincoln in her numerous soirees and receptions for the elite of Springfield.

In May of 1860, during the stirring sessions of the Republican Nominating Convention in Chicago, Lincoln discreetly remained in Springfield. Restless, he drifted in and out of the law offices of the Lincoln-Herndon firm, visited at the State-house, and loitered around home, reckoning his chances for the nomination. He knew that his friends and allies in the picturesque Lincoln headquarters in Chicago were using politics and rallies to promote his cause. Over the telegraph wires came the message: "We did it. Glory be to God." Lincoln beamed, shook hands all around, and hastened home to tell his wife. That night Springfield went wild. Friends and neighbors packed the Lincoln home in a happy celebration.

The following day some thirty-five distinguished Republicans, apprehensive over the selection of an unschooled backwoodsman as their standard bearer, got off the special train at Springfield and hurried to the Lincoln home. With stately dignity Lincoln met them at his front door and invited them into the north parlor. Rapid scrutiny by the crowd revealed a surprisingly fine home graced by a calm and pensive gentleman with a furrowed face and melancholy countenance. No man knew it then, but there stood the "man for the ages." In correct though ill-fitting clothes, Lincoln stood by a small center table which held a silver water pitcher, a photograph album, and a family Bible. With folded hands and slightly stooped shoulders he listened with a grave expression on his shaggy face while George Ashmun presented him with the letter of notification of his nomination for the Presidency and a copy of the Republican platform and made a short congratulatory speech.

Dignified and tall, his intelligent eyes lighting his countenance, Lincoln in simple words thanked the committee for the great honor, recognized his responsibility, and promised to respond formally when he had studied the platform. With cordial greetings and firm handshake he met each visitor. To break the ice, Lincoln asked tall Judge Kelley of Pennsylvania his height. Learning that Lincoln, at six feet and four inches, was the tallest man present, the Judge humorously remarked, "Pennsylvania bows to Illinois." Then Lincoln led the visitors to the south parlor where Mrs. Lincoln received them and served light refreshments and water. Later, Lincoln opined that the water seemed sufficient stimulant to satisfy them. After leaving the house, one committeeman remarked that he had met a gigantic rail splitter with the manners of a flatboatman and an ugly face, but he had met, too, a complete gentleman. Another called Lincoln a rough diamond.

It was a gala occasion for Springfield to honor the fellow-townsman who had won the nomination for the Presidency. The natives celebrated with cannon shots, fireworks displays, and a mass meeting at the courthouse; informal gatherings and receptions were held at the Lincoln home. The yard, the parlors, and the entire house buzzed with well-wishers. Local leaders predicted that enthusiastic campaigning was looming for the fall election of Lincoln as the American President.

The successful candidacy of Lincoln was promoted vigorously with a colorful campaign of pageantry, rallies, and speeches. Lincoln was called the "man who can split rails and maul Democrats." Log cabins, rails, and mauls were displayed with mottoes depicting Honest Abe's physical and mental prowess. Lincoln himself let his former speeches state his views across the nation, but he worked in the offices of the Statehouse and campaigned informally at home. From his porch he viewed parades and made speeches to enthusiastic crowds. In the final returns the humble frontiersman was elected over four rivals—one of them Stephen A. Douglas, who had split the Democrats with a North-South cleavage.

Abe Lincoln's peaceful prairie years were over, his turbulent Civil War years were in the offing. After his Presidential

National Capitol Building, Washington, D. C.

victory, Lincoln slipped off quietly to Coles County to visit his widowed stepmother and his humble friends of the past. Then he prepared to leave his home for Washington to serve his people. On a rainy day, February 11, 1861, the President-elect bade farewell to hundreds of friends who had come to bid him Godspeed. From the train platform he spoke one last time: "To His care commending you, as I hope in your prayers you will commend me, I bid you an affectionate farewell."

NATIONAL CAPITOL

Washington, D. C.

Today the magnificent Capitol Building which crowns Capitol Hill and cost more than $13,000,000 to build is one of the most beautiful edifices in the world. The classic structure, adorned with Corinthian columns and flanked by monumental wings of marble and stone, is glorified by its vast rotunda and crowned with an ornate dome. The huge dome itself is enhanced by a superb cupola on which a bronze statue of Freedom majestically stands twenty feet high. During kaleidoscopic years of history this democratic capitol has been a famous mecca for Americans who enjoy liberty and aliens who seek it. It has inspired pride in the achievements of each passing generation and buoyant hopes in rising young Americans.

However, the massive Capitol with its imposing environs is a far cry from the Washington of Abraham Lincoln's harsh times and of his arduous four years in the Presidency. Symbolic of the troubled unity of a torn nation, the unfinished dome cast shadows over the Inauguration of President Lincoln in 1861. The stark arm of a great crane swung awkwardly from the jagged dome. The bronze statue of Freedom destined to crown the stupendous edifice lay sprawled on the ground. Risen from a log cabin to a garish capitol, Abraham Lincoln emerged only to be confounded with news of seceding states, dissension in the ranks of the Union leaders, and a tottering Union.

The twelve-day trip from Springfield to Washington had been an ordeal. Lincoln's extemporaneous speeches from the train, his appeals at every whistle-stop for the preservation of the Union, and his patriotic addresses in large cities were the most taxing of his tumultuous career. While the special train rolled across New York, news came that Jefferson Davis had stood on the portico of the Alabama Statehouse and had taken the oath of office as President of the Confederacy. An actress, Maggie Mitchell, had danced on the Stars and Stripes! Wild counsel that the Confederacy and the United States must exist by peaceful compromise, or else be reunited by war, was thrust upon President-elect Lincoln. Reaching the Capitol with faithful detectives who guarded him against rumored plots against his life, Lincoln was haggard and worried. His black beard (which he was growing, so the story goes, at the advice of a young girl in Illinois, to make him look more dignified) accentuated his sober countenance, already solemn for the formal occasion before him.

On Inauguration Day, March 4, 1861, the weather was ominous and the crowd restless. By noon the clouds had broken and throngs lined the streets to view the procession and the ceremonies. On a temporary platform east of the Capitol Building the sedate principals appeared. Lincoln, dressed in a black suit and carrying his tall hat and an ebony, gold-headed cane, towered over President James Buchanan and Chief Justice Roger B. Taney. As Abraham Lincoln rose to deliver his address, Stephen A. Douglas reached out for the hat and cane; an aspirant to the Presidency held the togs of the great.

President Lincoln's Inaugural Address has been studied, applauded, and criticized, according to Northern or Southern views. He stated that he would respect constitutional provisions for the maintenance of slavery. "I shall take care, as the Constitution enjoins me, that the laws of the Union are executed in all states." On the eve of the Civil War Lincoln pointed out that physically speaking the states cannot separate, that political and commercial relations must continue.

"If the Almighty Ruler of nations, with His eternal truth and justice, be on your side of the North, or on yours of the South, that truth and that justice, will surely prevail, by the judgment of this great tribunal, the American people." He concluded with words of affection. "The mystic chords of memory, stretching from every battle field and patriot grave, to every living heart and hearthstone, all over this broad land, will swell the chorus of Union, when again touched, as surely they will be, by the better angels of our nature."

STATUE OF LINCOLN

Capitol Building

The splendid interior of the Capitol Building is enhanced by many statues, pictures, plaques, and paintings. The décor and the furnishings intrigue artists and inspire patriots. The lavish rotunda is a grandiose art gallery and a respected hall of heroes. Among this galaxy of great men the towering Lincoln left a stately mark on our land. Standing majestically in the rotunda is a marble statue of Lincoln, partially draped in a Roman toga, with head bent forward and eyes downcast, as if pondering the Emancipation scroll in his hand. This august statue, a remarkable likeness of a great American, was completed in 1871 by "a wisp of a girl," Vinnie Ream.

The novel story of the creation of this marble Lincoln is another historic page in the life of a celebrated American who inspired many who were privileged to work with him. Eager to make a portrait of the President, the eighteen-year-old Vinnie Ream obtained permission to study Lincoln at his convenience. At short intervals during the last five years of his life, Lincoln relaxed for the sittings, doing little business at these times and seldom seeing callers. Tucked away in a corner of the room, the talented young artist watched him. She never saw Lincoln as a story teller, but as a sad man with a "monumental melancholy always weighing upon his heart." Later, mourning with the nation over Lincoln's tragic death, Vinnie Ream obtained an endorsement signed by President Andrew Johnson, General Ulysses S. Grant, three cabinet members, thirty-one Senators, and one hundred and four Representatives for a Congressional award to make a statue of the martyred President. After much wrangling in Congress over the granting of a memorial commission to a mere, unknown girl, a joint resolution was passed by both houses and signed by President Johnson in July, 1866.

The coveted award provided for a model and a statue of

Statue of
Lincoln in the
Capitol Building,
Washington, D. C.

Abraham Lincoln to be executed at a price not exceeding $10,000, "one-half payable on completion of the model in plaster and the remaining half on completion of the statue in marble." Even a stinging rebuke from Mrs. Lincoln did not daunt Vinnie Ream. During the impeaching proceedings against President Johnson, some politicians wanted to use her studio room in the Capitol Building for a guard room, but they finally left her in her studio alone with her clay and plaster models. Accompanied by her parents Miss Ream completed her marble statue of Lincoln in Carrara, Italy.

On January 25, 1871, the unveiling of the Lincoln statue took place in the rotunda of the Capitol in the presence of President Grant, a large assemblage of government dignitaries, envoys of foreign nations, and many other spectators. Lincoln's old Illinois friend, Judge Davis, lifted the drapery, a flag sent from the weavers of France as a testimonial of respect for the American President.

Words of praise were spoken to Vinnie Ream about the statue which was "Abraham Lincoln all over." The statue was accepted as being "in the very manner of our noble patriot martyr." Many considered this marble Lincoln boldly and powerfully executed and believed "the unfathomable melancholy of the eyes" was faithfully indicated. A few days after the unveiling, the statue was taken to Statuary Hall where each state is represented by likenesses of two of its distinguished citizens. But eventually, in the belief that Abraham Lincoln belonged above all to the nation, the marble Lincoln was brought back to the rotunda where it stands today.

In his day the living Lincoln was as prominent in the Capitol as his likeness is revered in our times. While President Lincoln grappled with the oppressive problems of the War between the States, political dissensions in Congress, and distrust even among his cabinet members, he often sought counsel and found haven in the Capitol Building. Secretary of State Seward, who had expected to guide Lincoln, finally admitted, "the President is the best of us." Lincoln's line-etched features revealed his inner travail when he asked Congress for more recruits and more supplies to end the "People's War." His private secretaries, John Hay and John Nicolay, while handling his voluminous correspondence and his many clerical

demands, still found time to record his actions and to describe his painful reflection and his inspired decisions. Their notes became valuable publications later in his final absence and in their wise maturity. President Lincoln never ceased to believe in the principles of Thomas Jefferson and of those earnest founders who had built a nation on the premise that all men are entitled to "Life, Liberty, and the pursuit of Happiness."

THE WHITE HOUSE

For one hundred and fifty moving years the majestic White House has been the stately mansion of the First Family of our country. Rebuilt after the destructive War of 1812, often redecorated to suit the whims and needs of the incumbent Presidential family, the grand old structure waited with dignity and patience for the twentieth century to provide it with the necessary revamping and strengthening of the exterior and the rebuilding and refinishing of the interior. At intervals, work on the exterior has approximated several million dollars, and the complete reconstruction of the interior cost some five million. The rehabilitation of our Executive Mansion for enduring use has preserved essentially the expansive and classic exterior and many revered sections of the interior. The ensemble is an evolved and reinforced structure that preserves the sentiments and lore of the old, even as it provides for the unfolding future. The glorious White House is an integral part of our rich heritage of historic structures. It magnificently epitomizes the home, the center of family life upon which our democracy depends, and it represents to America and to the world the sacred and necessary nucleus of a God-fearing nation.

Into this grand home Abraham Lincoln and his family moved in 1861. As always, the White House, like a glass house, reflected the doings of the Lincolns with mirror-like accuracy. Social protocol regulating the numerous receptions, levees, state dinners, visits from the great and the lowly, and many social exigencies, in spite of the terrible Civil War, tempered Abe Lincoln's naïve disregard for convention, taxed Mrs. Lincoln's inherent social exuberance, and restrained the lusty tempo of the three growing boys. As war relentlessly tore the nation, President Lincoln's shrewd homespun philosophy,

formerly punctuated with droll jokes and tales, was now so-
berly applied to formal state papers, diplomatic sessions, dramatic public appeals, stacks of vital correspondence, and a
labyrinth of work for ending a horrible war. Even his daily
rides on horseback or in a carriage, exacted by "Mother" Lincoln for his health were punctuated with visits to hospitals
to cheer war victims.

With unconquerable spirit, Lincoln aptly remarked that
living at the Mansion was "piled high with difficulty." The
winning of the war became the all-absorbing, consuming task.
After the North had survived several serious invasion threats,
the South was slowly and painfully maneuvered into a defen-
sive and diminishing position. Despite his meager military
training, Lincoln had to direct military conferences in the Ex-
ecutve Mansion and sallied forth to persuade and pacify recal-
citrant generals and armies. He swapped and removed generals till he put the North on the offensive, and he named
General Grant to wear down the last tired forces of the daunt-
less General Robert E. Lee. Shrewdly, he refused to grant the
Southern leaders diplomatic recognition through any peace
conferences. Humanely and fairly he tried, but failed, to get
the North to offer, or the South to accept, partial compensation
for liberating their slaves and rebuilding the Union. Without
diplomatic entourage, President Lincoln personally drew foreign emissaries to the Executive Mansion to keep Europe
neutral in this internal war, and he sagaciously prevented
France and England from recognizing the Confederacy and
giving it the support necessary to win.

Waiting and hoping for Northern troops to take the offensive, and believing firmly that no state could lawfully with-
draw from the Union, President Lincoln, with a stroke of
genius, called his cabinet members into the White House for
a conference in September, 1862. Trying first to joke them into
a good humor before announcing his momentous decision, he
read aloud a funny travel story by Artemus Ward. Then to his
glum and critical cabinet of advisors, he calmly stated that he
had decided to use his war powers to free the slaves in the
rebellious states. He conceived as a uniform plan the preven-
tion of foreign recognition of the slave-holding Confederacy
and the proclamation to free the slaves that they might desert

their masters. By thus crippling the South he sought to re-unite the nation. In making the war a crusade against slavery, he simply stated that he would save the Union, if freeing all or part of the slaves would accomplish it. The famous Emancipation Proclamation, though it did not free the slaves in the North or border states, was a forerunner to the Thirteenth Amendment which President Lincoln relentlessly logrolled through Congress early in 1865.

Politics rode with war. In 1864, advising his fellow countrymen "not to swap horses midstream," President Lincoln was re-elected over strong opposition. His re-election was a heartening endorsement of his hopes, plans, and measures for preserving the Union and ending the Civil War.

President Lincoln, understanding human nature and recognizing his responsibilities, became a master in the art of war and the intricacies of statecraft. Reminiscent of his First Inaugural, the day of the Second Inauguration of President Lincoln was gloomy and foreboding. On March 4, 1865, the Chief Executive and his official party left the White House in a short procession and proceeded under low clouds along muddy streets to the Capitol Building. Significantly, the bronze statue of Freedom crowned the Capitol dome at last and stood guard over the mighty crowd that witnessed the Inauguration. To a hushed throng President Lincoln spoke briefly:

> Fondly do we hope—fervently do we pray—that this mighty scourge of war may speedily pass away. It still must be said! The judgments of the Lord are true and righteous altogether! With malice toward none; with charity toward all; with firmness in the right, as God gives us to see the right, let us strive on to finish the work we are in; to bind up the nation's wounds . . . to do all which may achieve and cherish a just and lasting peace among ourselves and with all nations.

Abraham Lincoln Room in the White House,
Washington, D. C.

ABRAHAM LINCOLN'S ROOM

The White House

In the restoration of the White House, the twentieth century halted the destruction of the passing years and promised a future. Necessity, patriotism, and sentiment prompted Congress to appropriate $5,000,000 for tearing out, reinforcing, and restoring the shaky interior of the White House. During the several years that President Harry S. Truman and his family occupied Blair House, the stupendous work of hulling, reinforcing with steel, and rebuilding according to elaborate plans was expertly and carefully consummated. The famous Lincoln Room, like many others including the Blue Room, the Red Room, the reception salons, and the dining rooms, intrinsically belongs to the historic structure.

The famous Lincoln Room has been faithfully reconstructed and all the cherished furnishings returned to their accustomed places. Posterity cherishes these relics of the last century, and eager guests at the White House appreciate the faithful preservation of a historic scene. The vaulted ceiling, the floral carpet, the simple draperies, and the antique furniture are truly Lincolnesque. The massive walnut bed, which was made long enough for Lincoln's giant frame, is ornate and inviting. The dust ruffles on the bed and the tables give the large room a homey touch. Only the telephone is a modern note in a century-old scene!

During his four trying years in the Executive Mansion, President Lincoln found sanctuary and rest in this master bedroom. Before the long mirror he often "spruced up" for the parades, receptions, and open houses. The careworn Executive obliged the stream of guests with greetings and handshakes, but he did prefer to browse in stocking feet in his office or in his bedroom—in striking contrast to Mrs. Lincoln, who was always elegantly gowned. Often he worked late with his secretaries John Hay and John Nicolay at reading, checking, and signing papers. With the "jobs husked out," he would check with the War Department for news before going to bed.

The White House could be restful, but it was not always comfortable. During summer evenings the lack of screens often gave Lincoln and his more informal guests excuses to punctuate their tales and jokes with resounding slaps at stinging insects. The gaslights that burned brightly in the Mansion lured bugs and challenged Lincoln, often garbed in a faded dressing robe, to fight the flying intruders with his old carpet slippers. One of Lincoln's musical favorites was "The Blue-Tailed Fly," and he often joined his cronies in singing the "Buzzing Ballad." In those soirées, patriotic airs, tender songs, and the simple melodies of Stephen Foster gave Lincoln keen pleasure in listening and singing. During the summers the Marine Band played stirring tunes on the White House lawn. He preferred listening to the music to the impromptu speaking he often had to do from the porch.

In spite of the War between the States and the shadows over the White House, the First Family was sometimes lively with the wit and drollery of Lincoln and his lusty boys. Robert recounted his experiences at preparatory school. Tad lisped as he told about his new uniform and his trips with his father to the battle fronts. Willie, who used to curl up in his father's lap to hear him read classics for children, became a fond memory to his bereft parents after he died of fever in 1862. For the next three years a twice-saddened First Family presided over the war-torn country.

The variety of Lincoln's interests gives an inspiring insight into his great character. During one of the Mansion receptions, the President honored the midget Tom Thumb and his tiny bride. The midgets were awed by the President of the gaunt face and big handshake. Lincoln graciously bent over to chat with them and thoughtfully provided high chairs for their dinner. The Lincoln boys were amused and amazed at the tiny couple. With his sons Lincoln often went to a play and sometimes indulged in good opera. During his few free hours his love of music was often pushed aside for a few moments with the masters of literature. The Holy Bible and Shakespeare were his forte. Lincoln frequently attended services at the Presbyterian Church with Mrs. Lincoln, and often took the boys to church after their Sunday-school services. Lincoln's spiritual concepts were ably expressed in his public addresses and informal speeches. His guide was the worn Bible that lay on his table beside the bed in his master bedroom.

SITE OF THE GETTYSBURG ADDRESS

Today the Soldier's National Monument in Gettysburg National Cemetery marks the place where President Lincoln delivered his immortal address in the dedication ceremonies on November 19, 1863. The massive gray granite pedestal of the monument rises sixty feet from a square base. This symbolic memorial in the center of a semicircular plot of graves is crowned by a colossal statue of white marble representing the Genius of Liberty. On the supporting buttresses are four flanking allegorical figures in white marble, representing War, History, Peace, and Plenty. Commemorating the states whose soldiers fought at Gettysburg, eighteen blue stars dotted around the tall shaft represent the Union and eleven gray ones designate the Confederacy. The cornerstone was laid on July 4, 1865, and the fine monument was dedicated on July 1, 1869.

By a series of transformations the bloody battleground at Gettysburg has been evolved into a beautifully landscaped national cemetery with appropriate headstones and memorials. Immediately after the battle, several thousand fallen soldiers were buried on the battlefield. Within six weeks attorney David Wills, agent of the governor of Pennsylvania, purchased seventeen acres of ground on Cemetery Hill and apportioned lots for the dead of each state. Contributions from each state aided in reinterment and memorializing. The removal of several thousand Confederates from the field was made several years later. In 1864 the Commonwealth of Pennsylvania incorporated the cemetery, but eight years after that it turned the burden of upkeep and the title of the cemetery over to the Federal Government.

The beautifully landscaped National Cemetery is a peaceful panorama in devout contrast to the sorrowful climax of a desolating conflict. During three terrible days some 80,000 Federal troops, commanded by General George G. Meade, defended Northern soil against the invading army of 70,000 Southerners, led by General Lee. On July 4, 1863, the two armies lay facing each other, exhausted and torn. After the bloodiest battle of the war in which men and officers fell in bleeding glory, General Lee and his brave men began the painful retreat that foreshadowed a lost cause. Inadvisedly,

Site of Lincoln's Gettysburg Address, National Military Park,
Gettysburg, Pennsylvania

General Meade failed to attack and cut off General Lee's retreat to the south and curtail the war. President Lincoln and his cohorts were grateful that Washington had again been spared, but disappointed that the grim battle had not been decisive. The President's gloom deepened when he learned that the Union losses were 23,186 men and that the Confederates had suffered 31,621 casualties—"all Americans."

On that same day Vicksburg surrendered to the amazing tactics of General Grant, allowing the "Father of Waters to flow unvexed to the sea," and this convinced the President that it would be General Grant who could finally exhaust General Lee's forces and end the devastating war.

Bloodier than Waterloo, as decisive a turning point as Yorktown, the battle of Gettysburg, with the brave men who died there, mutely clamored for consecration and commemoration. Even in the throes of the long war, the governor of Pennsylvania, assisted by the governors of several states, arranged for the Honorable Edward Everett to deliver the memorial oration on November 19, 1863. Since the Gettysburg cemetery was not at that time managed by the Federal Government, President Lincoln's acceptance of a formal invitation to attend the ceremony was unexpected. Forthwith, on November 2, a personal request was addressed to the President to take part in the program.

The Chief's visit to Gettysburg was an event that crowned sorrows. On November 18, at dusk, the Presidential train pulled into the small town. The President was escorted to the spacious home of Mr. Wills. The throngs milled about in the cluttered streets and serenaded the President.

On the following day at high noon, with thousands scurrying for vantage points to view the draped platform, the ceremonies were begun with a funeral dirge. The crowd stood for the opening prayer and listened while the Marine band played "Old Three Hundred." Then Edward Everett, a celebrated orator of the day, rose and "stood for a moment of silence, regarding the battlefield and the distant beauty of the South Mountain range." For two hours his fluted voice rose and fell as he rendered his memorized oration. With matchless gestures and arts of eloquence he reviewed the funeral customs of Athens, spoke of the purposes of war, described the three

Lincoln Speech Memorial, National Military Park,
Gettysburg, Pennsylvania

days of battle at Gettysburg, offered tribute to those who died there, and exhorted his audience to preserve the bonds of Americans. Upon the conclusion of his long address another song was sung.

Finally, President Lincoln arose, put on his spectacles, and unfolded a single sheet of manuscript at which he glanced briefly. In less than five minutes he slowly spoke the immortal words of "his little speech"—now revered as the Gettysburg Address. The Chief Executive had finished almost before the throng realized he had begun. The short pause was ended by tardy applause. A photographer was still adjusting his tripod when the President sat down. The crowd sang another hymn and heard the benediction.

Before leaving Gettysburg, President Lincoln drove over the battlefield and attended services in the Presbyterian church which had been used as a hospital during and after the battle. The President returned to Washington and the events of the dedication at Gettysburg became a sacred page in the history of our country which "under God . . . shall not perish from the earth. . . ."

LINCOLN SPEECH MEMORIAL

Gettysburg

The Lincoln Speech Memorial, reputed to be the only monument erected for an address in America, is a noble granite and bronze memorial to the immortal oration of a great man. With the passing of years the "few appropriate remarks" of President Lincoln at Gettysburg came to be accepted not only as an eloquent expression of the purposes of war, but as a masterpiece of the world's great literature. The essence of patriotic appeal, the Gettysburg Address has echoed on into two centuries. The Speech Memorial engraves Lincoln's memorable words into a glorious mark on our land.

Respectful and thoughtful planning finally culminated in the Congressional Act of 1895, which established a National Military Park at Gettysburg and provided for a fitting memorial to commemorate President Lincoln's glorious words on the battlefield. The contract for the bronze and granite monument was awarded in 1904, and the completed project, near the west gate of the National Cemetery, was dedicated in 1912. Against a backdrop of sturdy granite the bronze bust of President Lincoln is flanked by two bronze plaques that frame the famous words. Every school child in America is proudly familiar with the inspiring "little speech" of Lincoln, and many visitors annually pay tribute to the fine Speech Memorial.

President Lincoln's address evolved from the sentiments, stress, and experiences of the war years. In his Second Inaugural and in other notable speeches, the Chief Executive had strongly appealed for the preservation of the Union, appeals nobly and sagely reiterated at Gettysburg. After receiving the belated invitation, on November 2, 1863, to speak at the dedication services at Gettysburg, the President had ample time to prepare his "short, short, short" speech. Even after his arrival at the battle scene Lincoln put finishing touches to his words. The first page of the original text was written in ink on a sheet of Executive Mansion paper. The second page, possibly written or revised at the Wills' residence, was in pencil on foolscap. According to his secretary, John Nicolay, the few words in pencil at the bottom of the first page were added in Gettysburg. The second draft of the address was probably written on the morning of November 19, as some phrases, not in the first address, were later verified by Lincoln. Allegedly, the President held the second draft in his hand when he spoke. The first and second drafts are preserved in the Library of Congress. In all, five drafts were written by Lincoln, but his signature appears only on the fifth copy.

But the Gettysburg Address is more important than any legend or lore connected with it. In ten sentences of 268 wisely-chosen words, President Lincoln made a profound summation of national ideals and indicated a chart for the years ahead. Modestly the President underrated his eloquent words. He attributed the pause that followed his speech to apathy from a respectful audience that had been lulled by Edward Everett's two-hour oration, rather than to a hush that came from the lofty inspiration of his "few appropriate remarks."

Mixed printings and fuzzy editorials reduced contemporary appraisals. The big dailies printed Lincoln's speech, but generally as an appendage to Everett's oration. Country weeklies found Lincoln's terse remarks well suited to their limited space. Editorial comments usually followed political alignments. Republican editors praised the address, if they mentioned it. One Chicago paper blushed for Americans who read "the silly, flat, dishwatery utterances." The Massachusetts *Springfield Republican* recognized it as "a perfect gem, deep in feeling, compact in thought and expression."

Time has immortalized and fame has consecrated the "little speech" made by President Lincoln at Gettysburg. The words "under God," which do not appear in the first or second drafts of the address but which came to Lincoln while he spoke, have over the years added consecration to an eloquent appeal. Then as now, "this nation, under God, shall have a new birth of freedom—and [the] government of the people, by the people, for the people, shall not perish from the earth."

FORD'S THEATRE

The eighteenth century Ford's Theatre—now the Lincoln Museum—staged many dramas within its sturdy brick walls. Constructed in 1863, Ford's Theatre, with a seating capacity of seventeen hundred, was one of the finest theatres in the United States. The shocking assassination, on April 14, 1865, of President Lincoln by John Wilkes Booth was by far the most tragic and the most dramatic scene ever witnessed there, and Booth was the villain in its galaxy of actors.

After the national tragedy, the curtain fell on Ford's Theatre and it existed like a broken actor on a back street for many years. The War Department closed the Theatre immediately and public opinion opposed its reopening. When Mr. Ford threatened legal proceedings, the Government rented the structure and remodeled it into a fireproof building for storing Federal records. In 1866 an act of Congress provided $100,000 for its purchase, and various agencies of the War Department used it for many years. In 1893 a second tragedy befell the fateful building when three floors collapsed, killing twenty-two clerks and injuring sixty-eight others. The building was restored during the following year.

Across the street the William Petersen House, where President Lincoln died, has endured many changes along with

Ford's Theatre, now the Lincoln Museum, Washington, D. C.

Ford's Theatre. In 1896 the Federal Government purchased the Petersen residence for $30,000, and it was used for exhibiting the Osborn H. Oldroyd Collection of Lincolniana which Mr. Oldroyd had assembled from Springfield to Washington over a period of fifty years. Finally, in 1926, the Government acquired this Lincolniana for $50,000. Six years later the greater part of the Oldroyd Collection was removed to the Lincoln Museum. The old Ford's Theatre and the House Where Lincoln Died were restored and refurnished in the mode of 1865. Some of the rare furnishings of Lincoln's Springfield home adorn the Petersen house, though many have been returned to their original setting in Springfield.

So at long last, and in chastened remembrance, the bustling twentieth century has preserved Ford's Theatre as the Lincoln Museum and the House Where Lincoln Died as a memorable place for the public to visit. Periodically plans are formulated to restore Ford's Theatre as it was when Tragedy featured Death in 1865. However, only a diorama of the stage, with a recorded voice, now describes the tragic scene.

Honoring the martyred President and preserving priceless memorabilia of the last century, the exhibits in the Lincoln Museum are arranged chronologically to describe the story of Lincoln's life. Countless pictures and daguerreotypes of Lincoln, often a willing subject, with his mop of black hair and extraordinary face, have been collected and arranged for an avid public. Today the American flag flies from a third story window, a mark of the nation's veneration for the martyred President and a symbol of glory on the Lincoln Museum which hallows his memory and reveres his last hours.

In April of 1865, the red curtain had fallen on the tragedy of war. At long last the Civil War was ended and the torn nation was saved, but not spared sorrow. In a dramatic scene on April 9, 1865, General Lee surrendered to General Grant, and the other generals soon pulled down the curtain of conflict. Two days later the war-weary Chief, burdened with an entourage of detectives, toured the war-torn areas in and around Richmond, the vanquished capital of the Lost Cause. The President began to bind the nation's wounds. His hopes and plans for the compassionate reinstatement and liberal reconstruction of the late seceded states were being formulated over radical opposition. Between the bad war and the hopeful peace, the merciful Executive steadily applied his statecraft for the rapid rehabilitation of his beloved country.

On the evening of April 11, after his depressing visit to Richmond, the President made his last public utterance to a party of serenaders who had come to congratulate him on the successful closing of the war. In a short impromptu speech interspersed with characteristic anecdotes, the Chief Executive mentioned the problems of readjustment in the South and defended his proposed policy of treating the late Confederates in a charitable manner, in the hope of effecting a speedy reconciliation between the hostile sections of the unhappy country.

On the evening of Good Friday, April 14, the stage was set for the tragedy. The terrible Civil War was over and there was much to do. However, the exhausted leader felt he "must let up a bit." Ford's Theatre, featuring *Our American Cousin,* offered "some sort of change." On that fateful evening after a long day of official drudgery, President Lincoln with his wife and two young friends arrived late at Ford's Theatre. When the President appeared, the band struck up "Hail the Chief." The packed audience rose and cheered. The Chief bowed graciously and led his party to the President's flag-draped box above the stage. At about ten o'clock, while the President sat absorbed in the third act of the play, John Wilkes Booth, an actor and a fanatic, sneaked into the carelessly guarded booth and shot President Lincoln in the back of the head. In his long leap to the stage, the assassin caught his foot in the Treasury Guard flag which draped the Presidential booth and broke his leg. However, the dastardly actor dashed across the stage brandishing a dagger and exclaiming, *"Sic semper tyrannis!"* But John Wilkes Booth was the true tyrant; Abraham Lincoln was the innocent victim. The United States was irrevocably bereft.

Soldiers carried the unconscious Chief from Ford's Theatre across the street to the modest home of William Petersen. In the presence of his stricken family, his shocked cabinet, and sorrowing friends, the mortally wounded President lingered during a long night. At dawn on April 15, 1865, Abraham Lincoln gained peace—and immortality. The noble leader had gone to his great reward. To a sad world Edwin Stanton, Secretary of War, spoke the words which epitomized Abraham Lincoln's worth: "Now, he belongs to the ages."

The cowardly act of John Wilkes Booth and his sorry associates is true proof that villainy is costly. Booth's death in a burning barn and the punishment of his conspirators were poor retribution for the loss of Lincoln's notable and valuable life. The prostrate country suffered tremendously in losing his humble, brilliant, and compassionate services. History was enriched by a noble martyr. At the state services in the White House, spiritual condolences were extended to a sorrowing nation.

"Man is cut down as a flower. Yet Death may be swallowed up in victory."

LINCOLN MONUMENT AND TOMB

Springfield

Today an impressive structure in Oak Ridge Cemetery in Springfield memorializes the final resting place of Abraham Lincoln. The imposing shrine daily attracts throngs who pause to honor the Great Leader and admire the lavish memorial. Symbolically, the original monument, like Abe Lincoln himself, has been heightened, expanded, beautified, and glorified through many changing years. The erratic and grieved widow of the martyred President finally decided to pass up Arlington Cemetery and a site in Chicago for a "retired" place in Oak Ridge Cemetery in his old home town. Plans and work for a memorial and tomb to honor Lincoln began on May 1, 1865, four days before the funeral train from Washington arrived in Springfield, and continued apace until 1931.

In more years than Lincoln lived, the work of perfecting his sepulcher has been carefully and reverently continued. The Springfield committee of nine members, which had supervised the funeral arrangements, was later incorporated into the Lincoln National Monument Association, which started the construction of a "monument to the memory of Abraham

Lincoln Monument and Tomb, Oak Ridge Cemetery,
Springfield, Illinois

Lincoln." The day before the funeral train arrived, the committee opened books for subscriptions for the Memorial Fund. The Fund grew slowly from a total of $37 on the first day to large sums from state and national groups. By 1866 more than seventeen hundred Sunday schools had given $18,000 and the veterans contributed $28,000 to swell the total sum to $250,000.

Unflagging zeal and devoted service continued to build a worthy memorial. A "friendly competition of American artists" produced extraordinary designs for the memorial. Finally, Larkin G. Mead, Jr., of Vermont was awarded a contract for $70,000 to "mold, cast, and deliver" a statue of Lincoln, not less than ten feet high with four supporting groups representing the navy, infantry, cavalry, and artillery of the United States. The Association accepted a bid of $136,550 by W. D. Richardson of Springfield for the erection of the monument. In 1869 the ground was broken with appropriate ceremonies, and two years later the capstone was set on the central obelisk. In July of 1871 Tad Lincoln died in Chicago, and his body was placed in a crypt beneath the structure. In the fall of that year the metallic casket of Lincoln was removed from its temporary vault and reinterred in the sarcophagus chamber, alongside the graves of William and Edward Lincoln. In 1882 Mrs. Lincoln was buried there, filling the family plot, with the exception of Robert Lincoln who was buried in Arlington Cemetery in 1926.

In mid-October of 1874 the Lincoln statue was unveiled and the memorial was dedicated. Thousands of people visited the prairie capital and flags flew everywhere. The procession to Lincoln's tomb was two miles long. President Grant delivered a short address and was followed by other eminent friends of the departed President.

Since that day of dedication the monument has been rebuilt twice. By 1901 the central shaft had been elongated and the foundations reshored. After a grotesque attempt to steal the body of the martyred Chief, his metal casket was firmly sunk ten feet under the ground in a concrete vault. The reinforced cenotaph, surrounded by national flags and the flags of all the states associated with the Lincoln family, now bears the simple inscription "Abraham Lincoln—1809-1865." The bronze grilles at the openings of the chamber may be opened or closed to suit occasions.

At a total cost of one million dollars for building, rebuilding, and maintenance, the majestic shrine inspires veneration for the Great Leader and praise for its builders. Within the rotunda is a reduced replica of French's seated Lincoln. Along the corridors are eight bronze statuettes representing periods in his life. The marble walls, the flags, the bronze plaques bearing the words of the farewell to Springfield, the Gettysburg Address, and a sketch of Lincoln's life all contribute to the noble atmosphere of this revered shrine. Outside, the bronze groups of infantry, navy, cavalry, and artillery enhance the ensemble. The Mead statue of Lincoln with one hand uplifted and the other clasping the Emancipation Proclamation shows Lincoln as he looked in his last days, with furrowed and meditative face. Gutzon Borglum's heroic head of Lincoln is inspired and thoughtful. The entire reconstructed memorial was rededicated by President Herbert Hoover in 1931.

However, the magnificent shrine of today is a far cry from the prolonged state funeral and temporary interment of the martyred President. In April, 1865, his mortal remains lay in state for four days in the National Capitol. On April 19 private funeral services were first held in the East Room of the White House. Then the state funeral procession marched slowly down Pennsylvania Avenue to the Capitol Building where Lincoln was the first President to lie in state in the rotunda. Then, with a special car draped in black, a funeral train moved slowly across the miles between Washington, D. C., and Springfield, Illinois, stopping in large cities for services and permitting millions of Americans to view the martyred President. The most remarkable cortege ever seen in the United States blended sorrow and veneration for the loss of the great leader of the Civil War and the champion of democracy.

Abraham Lincoln, the President-elect, had spoken a sober farewell to his townfolk four years before, only to return as the martyred President and to lie in state for the services at the old Statehouse on May 4, 1865, before the burial at Oak Ridge. At the dedication of the memorial in 1874, Governor Oglesby pictured Lincoln as entering upon the Presidency "like one feeling his way amid precipices in the darkness of night." For the nation he spoke a noble epitaph:

> And now under the gracious favor of Almighty God, I dedicate this monument to the memory of the obscure boy, the honest man, the illustrious statesman, the great Liberator, and the martyr President, Abraham Lincoln, and to the keeping of Time. "Behold the image of the man!"

THE LINCOLN MEMORIAL

Washington, D. C.

The magnificent Lincoln Memorial in Washington, D. C., is a glorious shrine and one of the most beautiful buildings in the world. Standing at one end of the Mall and facing the Washington Monument, this temple of symbolic beauty and aesthetic perfection represents the noble spirit of Lincoln and is a superb accomplishment of the twentieth century. The builders of the Lincoln Memorial did not mar the effect of the Washington shaft, which pierces the sky, or of the Capitol Dome, which rises dramatically from the landscape, but rather they added to the architects' delight, the historians' mecca, and the people's inspiration. For four breath-taking miles along the famous Mall, into the rectangular colonnade of the Lincoln Memorial, up the Washington obelisk, and beyond the Capitol Dome to the circular Jefferson Memorial, throngs daily visit the imposing edifices, absorb the historic legend and lore of America, and are moved by patriotic inspiration.

For nearly "three score years" the reunited country waited for a worthy national monument to Abraham Lincoln's memory. Since 1867 a memorial had been urged and contemplated. Many concepts of it, noble and ignoble, faded until the twentieth century produced this handsome temple. Finally, on Lincoln's birthday, in 1911, President Taft signed the bill which created a commission to choose a site for the memorial and launch its construction. In 1915, during President Wilson's administration, the cornerstone was laid. In the course of seven years the commission held thirty-one formal meetings.

The Lincoln Memorial, Washington, D. C.

John Hay stated their objective: "The monument must stand alone, remote from the habitations of men, apart from the turmoil and business of the city, isolated, distinguished, and serene." The commission chose the site on the Mall and selected Henry Bacon to build a memorial of beauty and grandeur, Daniel Chester French to design and construct the statue and pedestal, and Jules Guérin to execute decorative murals. Only William Howard Taft and two other commissioners survived to participate in the formal dedication of the handsome edifice in 1922.

In pictures or on sight, Americans instantly recognize the magnificent Lincoln Memorial. Built on a high terrace and reached by wide steps, the fine building is 188 feet long and 118 feet wide. The great hall is surrounded by thirty-six majestic Doric columns which stand for the states of the Union when Lincoln was President. The names of those thirty-six states appear on the frieze and the emblems of the present forty-eight are inscribed above the columns. The classic structure is divided into three sections marked off by Ionic columns. The central chamber, which is open in front, houses the gigantic, seated statue of Abraham Lincoln by Daniel Chester French. The two side sections contain massive stone tablets on which are inscribed Lincoln's Gettysburg Address and his Second Inaugural Address. On the wall above the tablets are Guérin's descriptive paintings. The classic beauty of the shrine is enhanced by neat landscaping and a reflecting basin. The cost of the Lincoln Memorial was $2,900,000.

Memorial Day, May 30, 1922, was a great occasion in our national capital. On that fair day, the Memorial building and the Lincoln statue were formally dedicated and presented to the Government of the United States. Among the 3500 invited guests were many distinguished persons, departmental representatives, members of the diplomatic corps, and patriotic organizations. The vast multitude, spread over acres of ground, heard the dedicatory services over amplifiers. Chairman William Howard Taft of the commission, then Chief Justice of the Supreme Court, presided over the assemblage. Applause greeted arriving dignitaries, but the ovation of the day hailed Robert Todd Lincoln, who sat on the platform. The addresses were eloquent. Poetry and music filled the air.

Statue of Lincoln in the Lincoln Memorial, Washington, D.C.

In accepting the Memorial, President Warren G. Harding said, "Today American gratitude, love, and appreciation give to Abraham Lincoln this lone white temple, a pantheon for him alone."

At first the design and concept of the Lincoln Memorial caused some bickering. A few critics contended that classical structure adorned with Greek Doric and Ionic columns was not representative of a martyred President who was born in a log cabin and grew up on a frontier. Simple folk believed that "a tree is best measured when it is cut down." The specter of another war frowned on a monument to the war President of a divided country. One clergyman stated that it was "too early for painting, poetry, and sculpture to make the best of the materials which the Civil War properly furnished for the muses of the future."

But today the magnificent Lincoln Memorial is revered as an expression of American ideals. As a shrine of beauty and grandeur the Memorial inspires visiting millions to respectful silence and lofty thoughts. This Lincoln temple does not express the externals of the man, nor his humor, nor his manner, but "the qualities that made him great, the nobility of soul, the deep sense of honor, unselfishness, and self-sacrifice, the tenderness and the loving kindness are things that are unchangeable from generation to generation and command symbolical expression through the art of any time or mode." The Lincoln Memorial "does fittingly show forth the inherent nobility of the man it commemorates," and it symbolizes the eternal reverence of a great nation.

STATUE OF LINCOLN

The Lincoln Memorial

Even more celebrated than the classic Lincoln Memorial in Washington, D. C., is the monumental statue of Abraham Lincoln that sits within its columned portals. In pensive pose Abraham Lincoln, who preserved the Union through the travails of war, looks down the Mall past the shaft for George Washington, who forged the Union by war and peace, toward the column-encircled statue of Thomas Jefferson, who fashioned democracy restrained by law. Long ago Abraham Lincoln joined the stalwart ranks of the great. In his dedicatory address Chairman Taft aptly said, "The colossal figure of the Beloved . . . the work of Daniel Chester French, fills the Memorial hall with an overwhelming sense of Lincoln's presence."

The seated Lincoln in the Memorial daily inspires and awes the throngs who pay hushed tribute to the heroic personification of a great man. One of the largest marble statues ever made, French's seated figure of Lincoln is nineteen feet in height; standing, it would tower twenty-eight feet. It is composed of twenty-eight blocks of white Georgia marble, which were cut separately and perfectly fitted together on the huge pedestal in the central chamber. The width of the work, including the drapery over the chair, is nineteen feet. The firm pedestal of Tennessee marble is ten feet high. This noble statue of Lincoln was reverently made by the aging French, who had known and loved its subject.

The sculptured Lincoln reposes in a massive chair of state. The sides of the chair are blunted at the front with flat pillars on which are carved Roman fasces, symbolic of the power and indivisibility of the American Union. Lincoln's arms rest on the sides of the great chair; his powerful hands, moulded for action, extend over the fasces; his tense fingers seem to caress the thonged rods below them. The pose of the seated giant gives an impression of rest, but not the relaxation of the sprawling lawyer in his office back in Springfield. The President is calm, his head high, his body erect, ready for action. The furrows on his face, the sorrow in his eyes, and the solemnity of his countenance indicate a sober reverie on his four years of leadership in a terrible war for democracy, his abiding faith that "right makes might," and his spiritual understanding that all Americans "read the same Bible and pray to the same God."

A symbol of the man, the heroic statue of Lincoln appeals to the imagination and grips the vision of many people in various ways. To the simple folk he is the incarnation of their folk hero, Honest Abe who served the lowly, the Rail Splitter who was the champion of work. For the oppressed he is the epitome of Freedom, Emancipator of an enslaved race, Father Abraham to his humble followers. To the erudite Abraham Lincoln is versatility incarnate; he might have been a writer, an orator, or a poet, but he chose law and government. For the discouraged he is an image of inspiration; he was so often defeated and so rarely successful. To the patriot President Lincoln is the exemplification of statecraft, martyr to a great cause, the savior of the Union.

The living Lincoln of yesteryears is personified in this enduring marble image which is the most glorious mark of the man on our great land, for

IN THIS TEMPLE
AS IN THE HEARTS OF THE PEOPLE
FOR WHOM HE SAVED THE UNION
THE MEMORY OF ABRAHAM LINCOLN
IS ENSHRINED FOREVER

BIBLIOGRAPHY

BOOKS

Baringer, William E., *Lincoln's Vandalia*. Rutgers University Press, New Brunswick, N. J., 1949.

Bishop, Jim, *The Day Lincoln Was Shot*. Harper and Brothers, New York, 1955.

Bullard, F. Lauriston, *Abraham Lincoln in Bronze and Marble*. Rutgers University Press, New Brunswick, N. J., 1952.

Clark, Allen C., *Abraham Lincoln and the National Capitol*. Press of W. F. Roberts, Washington, D. C., 1925.

Gore J. Rogers, *The Boyhood of Lincoln*. The Standard Printing Company, Louisville, Ky., 1953.

Harper, Robert S., *Lincoln and the Press*. McGraw-Hill Book Company, New York, 1951.

Judson, Claire Ingram, *Abraham Lincoln*. Wilcox and Follett Co., Chicago, 1950.

Koral, Bella, *Abraham Lincoln*. Random House, New York, 1952.

Mearns, David Chambers, *The Lincoln Papers*. Garden City Publishing Co., Garden City, L. I., 1948.

Nevins, Allan, *The Emergence of Lincoln,* 2 vols. Charles Scribner's Sons, New York, 1950.

Randall, James Garfield, *Lincoln, the Liberal Statesman*. Dodd, Mead & Company, New York, 1947.

Randall, Ruth (Painter), *Mary Lincoln, Biography of a Marriage*. Little, Brown & Company, Boston, 1953.

Renne, Louis Obed, *Lincoln and the Land of the Sangamon*. Chapman and Grimes Company, Boston, 1945.

Sandburg, Carl, *Abe Lincoln Grows Up*. Harcourt, Brace & Company, New York, 1928.

Sandburg, Carl, *Abraham Lincoln;* The Prairie Years and the War Years, 1 vol. ed. Harcourt, Brace & Company, New York, 1954.

Sandburg, Carl, *Abraham Lincoln;* The Sangamon Edition, 6 vols. Charles Scribner's Sons, New York, 1946.

Sandburg, Carl, *A Lincoln Preface.* Harcourt, Brace & Company, New York, 1953.

Sandburg, Carl, *Lincoln Collector;* The Story of Oliver R. Barnett's Great Private Collection. Harcourt, Brace & Company, New York, 1950.

The Abraham Lincoln Association, *The Collected Works of Abraham Lincoln,* 9 vols. Rutgers University Press, New Brunswick, N. J., 1953-1955.

Thomas, Benjamin P., *Abraham Lincoln.* Alfred A. Knopf, Inc., New York, 1952.

Thomas, Benjamin P., *Lincoln's New Salem.* Abraham Lincoln Association, Springfield, Ill., 1954.

Williams, Wayne C., *A Rail Splitter for President.* University of Denver Press, Colo., 1951.

Magazines, Pamphlets & Manuscripts

Abraham Lincoln National Historical Park, Kentucky. United States Department of the Interior, National Park Service, Washington, D. C., 1955.

Appleton, Roy, *Abraham Lincoln, from His Own Words and Contemporary Accounts.* National Park Service, Historical Handbook No. 2, Washington, D. C., 1954.

Bennett, Hilbert, *Lincoln in Indiana.* The Rockport Democrat, Rockport, Ind., 1955.

Carpenter, Charles, *Capitol Guide to Springfield, Illinois.* Printed by the State of Illinois, Springfield, 1953.

Gray, Ralph, "Vacation through Lincoln Land." *National Geographic* (February, 1952), National Geographic Society, Washington, D. C.

Kelly, Edward James, *The Crime at Ford's Theater.* Action Publishers, Alexandria, Va., 1944.

Lincolnland. Lincolnland Promotional Committee, Santa Claus, Ind.

Lincoln's Boyhood Home, Knob Creek, Kentucky. Courtesy of Lincoln Tavern.

Lincoln Pioneer Village, City Park, Rockport, Ind.

McClure, Stanley W., *The Lincoln Museum and the House Where Lincoln Died.* National Park Service, Historical Handbook No. 3, Washington, D. C., 1953.

McClure, Stanley W., *Captions and Quotations of Exhibits in Lincoln Museum.* National Memorials and Historic Sites Division, National Park Service, Washington, D. C.

Meligakes, N. A., *Gettysburg, The National Shrine.* Gettysburg, Pa., 1948.

Nancy Hanks Lincoln State Memorial. Indiana Department of Conservation, Lincoln City, Ind., 1952.

New Salem State Park. Department of Public Works and Buildings, Division of Parks, Springfield, Ill.

Owen, Ira E., *New Salem Village.* Petersburg Observer, Petersburg, Ill., 1946.

The Abraham Lincoln Home. Department of Public Works and Buildings, Division of Parks, Springfield, Ill.

The Knox Idea. Knox College, Galesburg, Ill., 1956.

Three Lincoln Shrines in Illinois. Department of Conservation, Division of Parks and Memorials; issued by the State of Illinois, Springfield.

Tilberg, Frederick, *Gettysburg National Military Park.* National Park Service, Historical Handbook No. 9, Washington, D. C., 1952.

Truett, Randle Bond, *Lincoln, The Story of the Assassination.* Arlington, Va., 1949.

Whorton, Maurine, *French Diplomacy in the American Civil War.* Master's thesis, Washington University, St. Louis, Mo., 1925.

* * * * * * * *